A
GYPSY
IN
AUSCHWITZ

A
GYPSY
IN
AUSCHWITZ

OTTO ROSENBERG

As told to Ulrich Enzensberger

Translated by Maisie Musgrave

monoray

Originally published in 1998 by Eichborn Verlag, Berlin. Revised edition published as *Das Brennglas* in 2012 by Verlag Klaus Wagenbach GmbH, Emser Straße 40/41, 10719 Berlin, Germany

This edition first published in Great Britain in 2022 by
Monoray, an imprint of Octopus Publishing Group Ltd
Carmelite House
50 Victoria Embankment
London EC4Y 0DZ
www.octopusbooks.co.uk

An Hachette UK Company
www.hachette.co.uk

Distributed in the US by
Hachette Book Group
1290 Avenue of the Americas
4th and 5th Floors
New York, NY 10104

Distributed in Canada by
Canadian Manda Group
664 Annette St.
Toronto, Ontario, Canada M6S 2C8

ISBN 978–1–80096–112–8

A CIP catalogue record for this book is available from the British Library.

Printed and bound in the UK

10 9 8 7 6 5 4 3 2 1

Typeset in 11.5/18pt Plantin MT Pro by Jouve (UK), Milton Keynes

This FSC® label means that materials used for
the product have been responsibly sourced

This monoray book was crafted and published by Jake Lingwood, Mala Sanghera-Warren, Alex Stetter, Melanie Fitzgerald, Maisie Musgrave, Robert Anderson, Mel Four and Lisa Pinnell

Illustrations on pages 3, 4, 8, 28, 37, 38, 41, 46, 60, 100, 124, 125, 174, 182 and 199 courtesy of Archiv Landesverband Deutscher Sinti und Roma Berlin-Brandenburg, Familie Rosenberg.

Contents

Foreword

The history of the Sinti and Roma in Germany lurches between acceptance, marginalization and discrimination, but the foundation of the German Reich in 1871 marked an upsurge in their suppression and forced displacement. In 1929, this culminated in an agreement between the German states to grant a mandate to the Bavarian Zigeunerpolizeistelle (Gypsy Police) to coordinate all actions against Sinti and Roma, and from 1933 onwards, the SS integrated all of the resulting case files into its investigations into 'non-European alien races' in Germany.

Things deteriorated dramatically from late January 1933. Many of the orders that had been directed at the Jews also contained provisions that affected Sinti and Roma. The ban on employment meant that Sinti and Roma were prevented from pursuing a livelihood, leading to accusations that they were unwilling to work. From 1937, those who defied these orders could be sent to concentration camps under the Crime Prevention Decree. As early as 1935, the Nazis started setting up communal internment camps in some of the big German cities – first in Cologne, and later in Berlin, Frankfurt am Main, Magdeburg and Düsseldorf. Sinti and Roma were forced to live in inhumane conditions in these camps, under the supervision of the local police authorities. In Berlin, the police arrested around six hundred Sinti and Roma just before the 1936 Olympic Games, including my father and his family, and took them to the Berlin-Marzahn forced labour camp. Between 1936 and 1943 alone, 52 children and teenagers died as a result of the appalling living conditions there.

After the founding of the Racial Hygiene and Demographic Biology Research Institute, personal information relating to all Sinti and Roma at the Marzahn camp were collected under the direction of the doctor Robert Ritter and his assistant, the nurse Eva Justin. The law enforcement authorities would later use this information to assign individuals for compulsory sterilization and admission to concentration camps.

Large numbers of Sinti and Roma were deported to German-occupied Poland for the first time in May 1940. In autumn 1941, around 5,000 Roma were transported from Burgenland in Austria to the Łódź ghetto, which had been set up for Jews; others were taken to the Warsaw ghetto. On 16 December 1942, Heinrich Himmler, Reich Leader of the Schutzstaffel, or SS, and Chief of the German Police, issued a decree ordering the deportation to Auschwitz of all Sinti and Roma from the German Reich and Nazi-occupied areas. In early March 1943, almost all the inmates of the Marzahn forced labour camp were deported to the 'Gypsy Camp' at Auschwitz.

The SS intended to liquidate the Auschwitz-Birkenau Gypsy Camp on 16 May 1944, but their plan failed due to unexpected, and extraordinary, resistance from the prisoners. Soon afterwards, around three thousand Sinti and Roma were selected as 'fit for work' and transferred to other concentration camps. Around 2,900 prisoners remained in the camp, mostly the elderly, the sick and children: they were murdered in the gas chambers on the night of 2–3 August 1944. In total, around five hundred thousand Sinti and Roma fell victim to the Nazis' frenzy of racial hatred. My father was one of the few survivors.

Petra Rosenberg, April 2022

Chair of the Berlin-Brandenburg State Association of German Sinti and Roma; Chair of the Berlin-Marzahn Forced Camp Memorial

Chapter One

Since time immemorial – as far back as I could remember or anyone could tell me, at any rate – we had been a German Sinti family.[1] My father was a horse dealer and my mother a housewife, with a sideline in peddling goods and telling fortunes. I was born in Draugupönen, East Prussia, in 1927. My parents separated at around that time, so at the age of two or three months I was sent to live with my grandmother in Berlin. 'Of course, the boy can live with me,' she said, and that was that.

My sister Therese came later, followed by my eldest brother, Max, so the three of us ended up living with our grandmother. My second brother, Waldemar, lived with us briefly before going back to my father in East Prussia. My stepsister, the daughter of my father's first marriage, also lived with Father, in the Stallupönen and Gumbinnen area around Bialystok, right up against the Lithuanian border.

When I was five or so I went to stay with my father for a few weeks. He was a well-known figure, even among people in Berlin. He was about the height I am today – fairly short, in other words – but bigger, over 200 pounds. He sported a little goatee and a handlebar moustache twisted up at the ends. He was musical, too: he could play all sorts of instruments. People had plenty of good things to say about him, but he had such a fiery temper that he inspired a lot of fear, too.

Lots of Sinti people moved around constantly in their caravans, but my grandmother wasn't keen on that sort of life. We did move from place to place in Berlin, living on Weißensee, Rennbahnstraße, Feldtmannstraße and Müllerstraße, then in Pankow-Heinersdorf and later Altglienicke, but we never went travelling as such. Instead, we lived a simple life on privately rented sites. The place we stayed on Feldtmannstraße was set back from the street and

Otto (second left) with his mother, Luise Herzberg, and his
siblings Waldemar, Max und Therese in Berlin, *c.*1930

Hermann Herzberg, Otto's father.
He was killed in the Białystok Ghetto around 1941.

had its own gateway, with at least ten caravans pitched inside. If we no longer fancied staying on a site, we would simply borrow some horses from our kinfolk or acquaintances, hitch them up to our caravans and go. People would sit together around the fire of an evening, drinking a bottle of beer and having something to eat, and then at the crack of dawn next day we children would hear the horses on the cobbles. We would help to fasten the ropes and harness the horses. Then came the caravan, usually with a stable-type door at the front or a window that you could open. A cart with low sides was hitched up to the back, for the people who were coming along to help us to use on their way back later.

As soon as we arrived, we unharnessed the horses and rewarded them with chopped straw with crushed fodder and oats mixed in, and then another bundle of hay. We would sit down to eat, before manoeuvring the caravans into place and setting them up. When evening came, we settled in while the others rode back in their low-sided cart, with a kerosene lamp to light the way.

The sides of the cart were fitted with lengths of iron

or wood with slots, into which crosspieces and planks were inserted, so that they were suspended about one and a half metres above the ground. Iron brackets were attached, or – even better – freshly cut birch or hazel branches, folded, tied and woven until the sides were as solid as can be. A tarpaulin was spread over the top and boxes for odds and ends and for sitting on built in on either side.

Our horses were always very well treated. When the time came to barter or sell a horse, the job of showing it off would be given to one of the sharper boys. I did it quite a few times. Pulling off the deal would earn us a tip from the buyer – ten, maybe twenty, pfennigs or so. If the horse dropped its head, you'd have to jiggle the reins to get it to look up nicely.

The women made a living peddling goods and telling fortunes, while the men wove baskets, crafted tables and chairs from root timber and decorated cabinets. Later, all of that was banned; they were forced into compulsory labour and received welfare payments instead.

My mother's family was highly respected among the Sinti. My grandmother's brothers were clever chaps, especially my Great-Uncle Anton and Great-Uncle Albert. They were avid readers, keen riddle solvers and could write beautifully, with perfect spelling. They could build entire chapels to Our Lady with root timber, or use it to decorate caravans, with nothing but an axe and knife as tools. Their talents knew no bounds. Their brothers would pitch in by putting up scaffolding or carving wooden pegs.

The Rosenbergs dealt with the authorities and were the go-to experts if anyone needed to know anything. My grandfather could put together any necessary documentation. If someone died, the brothers would make the arrangements for the funeral and pass around a hat to collect money. Then they'd head straight to the pub and drink the lot away. One of the brothers was a familiar face at the coffinmaker's: 'Make it how I tell you to, then when you're done, tell me how much it is, and I'll pay you then.' And that's exactly what happened. He would pay out the money that they had drunk away, and the matter was settled. It wasn't exactly by the book, but people did what they needed to for each other when it mattered.

Most of the people from the site went out to work.

Florian Rosenberg and Luise Herzberg, after 1945

Some would busk; others would strap on a pannier and sell haberdashery or leather goods. There were a few slackers, though, who did nothing but loll about strumming their guitars. My Uncle Florian, who was immensely strong, worked carrying colossal loads on his back at construction sites. There were no mechanical lifts back then, of course. Some 150 pounds or more of bricks were stacked in a rack which he then hoisted onto his back and could heave up three ladders.

We played a lot of card games at our camp – skat, Silesian lottery; standard German games. We children liked playing a game that we called *Panschbara*, with five rocks. You had to draw a grid in the dirt with a stick and try to throw a bicycle chain into it. The youths in the camp kept active, lifting weights with old carriage axles or playing football with a makeshift ball fashioned by stuffing their jackets into an old jumper and sewing it up.

Our celebrations were especially fun: people would play together on their guitars and violins; there would even be a double bass and accordion. There were some wonderful singers among us, including my brother

Max, who was always called upon when there was something to celebrate.

We were like one big family in those camps. Everyone knew each other; you never came across anyone who was a complete stranger. People would freely share their sugar, salt and onions, and if women were out late, the others would rustle up sandwiches for their children.

My parents only showed their faces around there occasionally. If they came by, it tended to be late in the day, when I was already tired and drifting off to sleep. I still have a memory of sitting in my mother's caravan while she cooked some macaroni. As I sat there, waiting for my dinner, I fell asleep. When I woke up, I was back with my grandmother. Later, after the concentration camp, I brought it up and teased her about it: 'Some kind of mother you are! Do you remember the time I was in your caravan and you made me macaroni, but I fell asleep and never got to eat it?'

'Oh, I remember, all right,' she said. 'You fell asleep, so I gave your dinner to your grandmother for you. A great big plate of it! I said to her, 'You'd better take this macaroni for him, otherwise when he wakes up he'll go around saying that I made him go hungry.' 'It's true: I was always hungry as a boy, but if I wanted something to eat, I needed to work long and hard for it.

I was closer to my grandmother than to my own parents. Wherever she went, she always took me with her. She brought me up and told me of the things that had happened before my time. In the evenings, the older ladies would get together around the fire and tell all sorts of stories from the past about relatives and people who had died. There would be old fairy tales, too, rich and wonderful stories, sometimes with a touch of malice. I would sit there, enfolded in my grandmother's apron, and listen in to everything they had to say.

'Mami!' I probably said – she wasn't *Oma*, or 'grandmother', to me – 'Mami, what was it like back then? Were you around?'

'Yes, my boy.' Her voice was so soft and kind.

'Tell me what happened!'

'Oh, don't keep asking questions, my boy. I've got a headache.'

Naturally, I would ask, 'What's a headache? Mami, tell me what it's like to have a headache?' When I was a little boy, I always wanted to have a headache so that I would know how it felt, but I never did. Not back then, anyway; later I had them, of course.

She never took any medication, apart from maybe Hoffman's Drops if she felt nauseous. Whenever she had a headache, she would soak a rag in vinegar and tie it around her head. When the sun came down, she would take a large rhubarb leaf, press it against her forehead and tie her shawl around it, to protect her from the sun.

It was genuinely a very peaceful existence. Paul von Hindenburg was president of Germany back then; I remember his profile on the big five-mark coins.

Our final move was to Sandbacher Weg in the Altglienicke-Bonsdorf district. My Uncle Florian (the construction worker) probably arranged it all for us. We rented an apartment there, plus a plot of land where we could park our covered wagon. A whole load of us lived there – me, my grandmother, my brother Max and my other brother, Waldemar; from time to time, my sister Therese and Uncle Florian, who parked his caravan there, too, and his family, along with my Aunt Camba and her husband, Paul, both of them still very young. Over time, we were joined by others, including the Krapp family – a Bavarian man who had married a Sinti woman, and their children. They traded in scrap, screws and copper. We lived there for several years.

We built little wooden coops and hutches for our chicken and rabbits. The kids were tasked with keeping the yard clean, sweeping the street and gathering scrap paper and discarded cigarette butts. Occasionally, the landlord would give us an ice cream or sweets for doing our chores.

While we were living in Sandbacher Weg, we also started school. I experienced my share of discrimination back then, too, but you take it differently as a child. I fought back against the children who tried to put me down. I always wore clogs, presumably because we didn't have the money for proper shoes. Those wooden clogs looked so tough that they actually earned me some respect.

The other children liked to strap their satchels onto their fronts, so that they were on their chest, and play aeroplanes. In their games, they would barge into me and call me names – 'dirty gypsy', that sort of thing.

One day, I retaliated by beating up a boy with my clogs. The only problem was that this boy happened to be the son of a policeman, who marched into our classroom the next day with his son. I was rooted to the spot with fear. Our teacher, Herr Kühne, seemed a giant to a boy of my size, towering six feet or so. He called me up to the front for the policeman to cross-examine me. Why had I done this to his son?

'Because he called me names,' I said. 'He shouted "Gypsy scum!" at me. We got into a fight. He punched me and hit me with his satchel, so I took off my clog and let him have it . . .'

'All right, that's enough.'

The policeman had a word with the teacher as I took my seat again. I was sure that the policeman was going to lock me up; children have a very black-and-white idea of what the police do, after all. But he didn't. I could hardly believe my luck. Later, Mr Kühne called me over and took me to task: I mustn't ever do such a thing again. If I had a problem with anyone, I had to come and tell him, and he'd sort it out. Things calmed down a lot after that.

My cousin Oskar, who also lived in Altglienicke, went to the Bonsdorf school with me; we Rosenbergs sat in the same row, and as schoolbooks were scarce, we shared a reading book. When it was time to read, we would do it together, competing with each other. Looking back, it was a fun way to learn.

I was friends with Christa Kühne, the teacher's daughter, while Oskar was friends with a girl named Gerda Nitschke. We weren't nearly as well-to-do as the teachers' daughters, of course. They got milk and cocoa to drink. Sometimes, the Quakers would give us bread rolls in school or we'd get some milk, but it wasn't a regular thing. The girls would let us drink from their cocoa or milk bottles, turning the straw the other way up, or give us some of their breakfast; they were nice like that.

One day, things took a turn for the worse. When we went to shower, my classmates started making a thing of my darker skin. 'Come on, let's grab Otto and scrub him whiter.' They thought it was hilarious, but I didn't see the funny side. And my skin stayed put, no paler than before.

After school, we often took a detour on the way home. In Adlershof, fairly close by, there was a large church and convent of nuns. When we turned up there, one of the elderly nuns, Sister Riecke, would invariably greet us with, '*Grüß Gott*, dear children. Would you like some soup?' We answered a resounding yes. She gave us a bowl of soup and a slice of bread. Even though the country was still at peace back then, moments like these were wonderful for us children. We would always stop by there before eventually making our way home.

I was entranced by the roadworkers laying down asphalt and boiling tar, and liked to linger a while, watching and chatting to them. I could usually even cadge a sandwich from them, while they asked me what I did and where I came from, and I answered willingly.

At the back of our land, in the woods, lived the Ingashevsky family, who were connected to the church. They had a lovely spot, where we would go for prayers and to receive religious instruction.

It's all such a long time ago now. In those days, we lived in peace.

My grandmother was a wonderful woman, so sweet and kind. Everyone liked her, she could get on with anyone, and she was always worrying about our welfare. We weren't rich, but we had what we needed. And even though our socks often had holes and she was constantly darning them, patching trousers or mending shirts and collars, we were always clean and well turned out; we weren't an easy target for jibes about 'dirty gypsies'.

For my part, I always tried to be helpful: I knew that if you do something for someone, you might get something in return. And it always paid off, even if I only came away with a sweet. As far as I was concerned, that was reward enough.

Chapter Two

At four or five one morning, we were woken with a jolt by the Stormtroopers and the police. 'Quick, get dressed! Move it!'

It was total mayhem. In all the commotion, we noticed that our local policemen, whom we knew by sight, were there, too. We were loaded onto trucks. Our covered wagon was also brought along. How did these people have the right to remove us from a private camp?

We were carted off to Berlin-Marzahn or, as it was officially known, Berlin-Marzahn Rastplatz. Yes, they called Berlin-Marzahn a rest stop.[2]

This was in 1936, before the Olympic Games. I had just turned nine.

So there we were. When we arrived, the grass was so tall that us kids could get lost in it. It all got cut down, dug up and levelled, with stones lifted in to fill in any potholes. By the time they'd finished with it, the whole site was completely flat. They just dumped us in this place. We had been detained; everyone was forbidden from leaving. The earth was scored with ditches, and the surrounding land was a sewage farm. A constant stream of wagons pumped liquid manure into the ditches. You can imagine the smell. Left to our own devices, we would never have pitched up in such a spot, not least because our laws forbid it. But we were forced to do so now. Apart from holding us there, no one was interested in our welfare: 'Right then, let's see how you get along here.'

There are tower blocks there now. If I visit the site today, I can only get my bearings by looking at the railway tracks, the level crossing and the cemetery. Trains went right past the camp on their way to Werneuchen.

It was about a 20 minute walk from Marzahn village to the camp. From there the road continued on to Falkenberg.

So there we all were: my grandmother, my brother Max, my sister Therese, my 14- or 15-year-old Aunt Camba and me. Oskar ended up there, too, followed by his father, my Uncle Florian, my mother's brother, along with Bodo, Oskar's little brother, and his sister and another brother. There were four children in his family, just like ours. Oskar's sister – Jenny, her name was – later died in Marzahn. More and more people arrived, and with them infections and diseases increased. People were living in shacks hastily assembled from corrugated iron. If they wanted any form of shelter at all, they had to construct it themselves, as there was absolutely nothing there.

Actually, I tell a lie – there was a police hut there, and a school hut, as we were barred from attending the public primary school. Normal school was now a thing of the past.

The big school right beside the village church in Berlin-Marzahn was off-limits to the likes of us. We only had the one teacher, and although there were several classes, they were crammed into two rooms: one for the really little ones, and the other for the rest. Some of the books came free, but we had to pay towards others. We had exercise books for working out sums and for writing, a reading book and an arithmetic book each, and that was it. Not a lot of learning went on.

We were allowed to go shopping in the village, though. There was Herr Drilling the milkman, a Herr Haase's grocery store, which sold coal, and the blacksmith. We knew everyone there, and they knew all of us. There was a bus stop outside the church, too, so we could take the bus there. Once everyone had received their papers and everything was set down in writing, we were permitted to leave the site. We could even go into the city, but we always had to return to the camp.

Whenever we went out, we had to walk past the police hut, which had a huge window that allowed them to keep a lookout over the site. We had to go past the policemen. Most of the time, we would say hello, as we knew them, and we did the same when we came back. Other paths that would have got us to the shops or even the train station more quickly were strictly out of bounds. Anyone who headed down one of those paths would have dogs sent after him, get beaten up and probably have to pay a fine.

I remember that fetching fuel for the fire meant a 20 minute walk. We could get coal from Willi Haase, in sacks weighing twenty-five to fifty pounds. I'd sling the sack across my shoulders and set off, but – as a boy of just nine or ten – I had to make frequent stops.

Fetching water, wood, coal . . . I certainly had my work cut out for me. Sometimes I would make three or four trips from the camp to Marzahn village. The woman who worked at the baker's always quizzed me, 'What can I do for you today, my love? Did you forget to wash your face again?'

Later, a Herr Fuhrmann started selling milk at the camp. Walter Schwarz eventually opened a grocer's shop there, too, and did good business.

I would go out to get milk in the depths of winter, trudging along for half an hour, my hands ready to drop off. Sometimes, I'd start feeling really sorry for myself, which pained my grandmother. She would often get into quarrels with other people, especially if they accused me of causing mischief. She would ask me, 'Tell me truthfully now, did you do it?'

'No, Mami,' I would say. 'It wasn't me.'

I never, ever lied to my grandmother. If you love someone that much, you always tell them the truth. She would dig in her heels: 'It wasn't my son! I know it wasn't, because if it had been, he would have said so.'

If I really had been up to no good, I would admit it to her. She would boom, 'Right, get in here!', all bossy and indignant. Once I was inside, she took out a carpet beater or a slipper, slapped it against something a few times, and whispered to me, 'Go on, yell!' I would let out some anguished howls. For all the people outside knew, she was really letting me have it, but she actually never punished me, not once.

At one point, some Turkish Sinti arrived, bringing with them a little circus, complete with horses, a few monkeys that they would dress up and had trained to hold out their hat when they went peddling their wares, and brown bears that danced to the beat of a tambourine. I made friends with one of the Turkish girls, Katharina, even though she spoke nothing but Turkish. She'd slip me a few pfennigs every now and then.

One of the monkeys could do backward leaps, somersaults, the full works. Once it ambushed me. I was going to see Katharina and happened to pass close to his cage. He was on a chain, but I was near enough that he managed to grab onto my head. He pushed me to the floor and began picking over my scalp, looking for lice. I couldn't get free; there was nothing for it but to call for help: 'Katharina, Katharina!'

On one occasion, my brother Max brought me an old Prussian spiked helmet. I cleaned and polished it until it gleamed. In those days, I used to play with another boy my age from a Roma family. He had a little dog. One day, my pal turned up in a military uniform, with a helmet, swastika, storm strap and sabre – the complete outfit. I thought he looked great and only wished I had the same.

We celebrated Christmas in our way: everyone tried to make something to give to others, to spread a bit of cheer. One evening, when the sun had already gone down, St Nicholas, dressed as a bishop, came to the camp, accompanied by a donkey and a dwarf. He wore a proper mitre and held a crosier, and went around visiting the children. The donkey was carrying a pack, from which every child was given a little bag containing an apple and a few sweets. The bishop greeted each child and laid his hands on them in blessing, me included. It was a huge moment for me. I was still pretty small for my age back then. I looked up at him and hesitantly gave him my hand. His was so nice and soft in its huge glove. It was a moment of pure joy. And then to get the little bag, too – even greater bliss.

The camp caused a great deal of curiosity: lots of people would come and take photos, and on a few occasions, they sneaked into the camp itself. The police were there in an instant to chase them away. 'Get lost!'

The Catholic nuns and missionaries from places like the Convent of Christ the King on Strausberger Platz always found a way to help us, though. No masses were held in Marzahn, but we sang hymns, and the nuns and priests would explain pictures of Jesus. Of course, I have these wonderful memories of them, but it does also have to be said that the Catholic and Protestant churches both turned over their registers to the Nazis, so ultimately they contributed towards the persecution of the Sinti and Roma.

We children paid regular visits to the Convent of Christ the King, as we were taught the catechism there every Friday evening after school. We could even stay the night there if we wanted; we were fed and could sleep in a dormitory. But we had to go back to the camp on Sunday.

There was Father Petrus, Brother Williges and Brother Bonifazius, who had a massive hump. All lovely men. The priest, a man named Trüding, instructed us in the catechism and the Catholic faith until it was time for us to make our First Holy Communion. They made us special outfits for the big day: sturdy-heeled wooden clogs and a suit with a white detachable collar. We loved being at Christ the King. The food was so delicious, and after school or for supper there was always a sweet, scrumptious soup served in a big mug, with baked or fried dumplings to go with it. When I cast my mind back, I can still conjure up the taste, even though I've never had such things since. The food alone was enough to keep us going back time and time again.

Otto's brothers, Max and Waldemar, at their First Holy
Communion, Altglienicke, Berlin, *c*.1934

Later, they said that if we wanted to stay there – times were bad, after all – it would be a good idea for me to become an altar boy. I made a start by learning a smattering of Latin, for the prayers at the foot of the altar: 'Et introibo ad altare dei'. I was on the verge of doing it. If things had gone on the way they were, without the war, I might well have stayed at Christ the King and I think that I might even have become a priest. But, of course, we'll never know.

Then came the day when the race researchers Dr Ritter and Eva Justin visited the camp.[3] They went from hut to hut and caravan to caravan systematically, completely focused on their goal. They would give people a bag of coffee and say, 'Let's have some coffee, and then we'll get started!'

They asked them about their background, where they came from, their parents, their grandparents, and so on. Some people could give that information readily, but others, especially the older folk, didn't know or recall much at all. I remember one big, stocky old lady – she must have been at least 80 – who couldn't come up with the goods and had her hair cut off in punishment. Terrible, when you think about it.

She probably didn't tell the truth or give Miss Justin and this Dr Ritter exactly what they were looking for; instead, she ran off and hid on Falkenberger Way. The police helped track her down and hauled her back in, which was when they chopped off her hair. Can you believe it, a woman of that age? When they were done with her, her hair stood up from her scalp in short spikes. They tipped icy water over her and made her stay standing out there, in the middle of winter. As I recall, she died within three days. Those were the kinds of things they did! I didn't see it happen, but I saw the woman after she was dead, with her little tufts of white hair. She was buried at Marzahn Cemetery, in a kind of tin crate, not a proper coffin.

The graves of Sinti and Roma who died during this period – including little Jenny – are still there today, but a lot of them have been levelled. Only the Sinti stones that we have placed there mark the spot. We meet there every second Sunday in June.[4]

Eva Justin and Dr Ritter paid our family a visit, too. It was all 'When?' and 'Where, where, where?' We told them what we knew. They made their enquiries all over the place, including at school. Eva Justin said,

'I'd like Otto to come by the Institute of Anthropology after school.' I dutifully went along. 'Sit yourself down here,' she said. 'Now, look at all these beads! Why don't you pick them up?' A piece of wire with a thread attached was placed in front of me. 'Make a necklace out of them.' I threaded various beads onto the string. 'Show me! Oh, beautiful!'

She made constant notes. Then she gave me a puzzle game, a board with holes that you had to manoeuvre a ball through. She showed me pictures, too: children running away, a broken windowpane, a man coming out of his house, him catching one of them. I remember it clearly. I was supposed to explain what was going on. I did everything that was asked of me.

Afterwards, she gave me a ride on her bike, with me sitting on the pannier rack. We rode down Unter den Eichen and over a bridge. She lived in a house on the corner of Curtiusstraße with her mother. I was given a room and a little bed – a heavenly bed, for me back then – to sleep in. She gave me food and drink, too. It was like something out of a dream. She acted so kind and sweet towards me.

Only later did I realize that she had just been performing a test on me, and then I saw the whole episode in a different light. It would have been better if she had given me a beating; I could have processed it a whole lot better. To this day, I still ask myself how she could have done it, while acting so nice? Things like that end up weighing on you more than any punishment.

After that, I helped out at the institute for quite a while, and I did it well. I came by once or twice a week to glue in slides. I didn't get paid for it, although I probably got the money for my fare.

Eva Justin's mother was a wonderful woman – at least, she was a great cook, so as a hungry young boy that put her high in my estimation. I have a very clear memory of her serving up some kohlrabi for me. I was familiar with uncooked kohlrabi, but I'd never come across it cooked. As it still had the woody bits, I refused to eat it.

'Very well, but if you don't eat it now, you'll have to eat it later, or tomorrow.' The next day, it was put down in front of me again. I knew I had to eat it, as otherwise I wouldn't be given anything else. Luckily, there was a bottle of Maggi seasoning on the table, so I doused the kohlrabi in it. 'See, that wasn't so bad, was it?'

When someone treats you kindly, but later you find out that they did it just to . . . well, it's hard to come to terms with it. I can't explain it any other way than that she didn't like me as much as she made out. Or perhaps she did, but it didn't stop her doing her work. I have no idea. I never spoke to her after the war, although she went on practising with Dr Ritter in Frankfurt.[5] Personally speaking, I couldn't have painted her in a bad light. How could I? If someone acts like a good person, you can't really say anything bad about them.

One night, I suddenly found myself dreading going to sleep in that room.

'What are you afraid of?'

'I can't put it into words,' I said. I was probably imagining ghosts.

And then there were all those glass cabinets thronged with monkey heads and skeletons at the institute. I didn't want to go in those rooms, but she locked me in. I was in there for half an hour, maybe even an hour. I shouted in terror, and I was furious, too, of course. Perhaps it wasn't such a long time after all, but it certainly felt like it to me. Then she came and unlocked the door.

'Surely you're not scared now? You know they can't do anything to you – there's no need to be frightened.' Maybe she wanted to calm my fears, but I was scared all the same.

Chapter Three

In 1938, the police or the SA – I can't remember which – came back. They gathered up all the young men and drove them away on trucks to Sachsenhausen in Oranienburg.[6] My Uncle Paul – the husband of my mother's sister – was among them. Most of the men were sent on to other camps. A handful returned to Marzahn; most did not.

My uncle had been tasked with slicing bread in the bakery at Sachsenhausen and came back with a nasty injury and his hand all wrapped in bandages. 'I mustn't breathe a word,' he would say. 'If I let anything slip, they'll come for me again.' Gradually, though, he did start opening up about what was going on in Sachsenhausen. There was fear, of course, even then. We were used to adults warning, 'If you kids don't start behaving yourselves, you'll be sent to the *Konzertlager*!' The concert camp, that's what they called it. It had a jolly ring to it.

By now, foundations had been laid and huts brought in. These old Wehrmacht huts were split down the middle, with a family living in each half. We were assigned to Hut 28a. My brother Max, my sister and I now lived there with my grandmother, my Great-Uncle Anton and my young Aunt Camba.

I rarely quarrelled with my sister; at most we'd have the occasional spat. The same went for the whole community. We were never hit at home, only occasionally by our other relatives. They should have stuck to slapping their own kids, not us. As I had been brought up by my grandmother, without a father or mother, everyone thought they knew what was best for me.

An infirmary was added behind the police huts for women to deliver their babies. The women would stay there until they were ready to come back to us. A room adjoining the infirmary was known as the Welfare Office, and people would go there when they were

Otto's Uncle Albert (wearing cap), Aunt Camba (left) and
sister Therese (centre), Berlin-Marzahn camp, *c*.1940

Otto's grandmother Charlotte (right) with her siblings,
Berlin-Marzahn camp, *c.*1936

out of work. One of them was old Uncle Pipper, who had previously earned a livelihood busking around the city with his zither. I remember that he always refused to go on the bus, saying, 'You won't catch me on one of those death traps. I won't set foot on them.'

My grandmother also went to this Welfare Office, like all the other older women. I don't know how much they got exactly, but it would have been a few marks a month.

There was a Herr Huckauf there, who was a complete yes man around those in charge. Then there was Herr Schukalla, with his red face, who liked to throw his weight around and make everyone scared of him. Yet one day he got me out of school and took me to Lichtenberg, where he bought me a pair of plus fours, those baggy-kneed trousers, new shoes to go with them and a matching hat. That happened sometimes: people wanting to do us a good turn. You can imagine how proud I was, going to school like that. I looked like a brand-new person in all my finery.

Schukalla used to bark out orders like an angry dog. My uncle ran into him again after the war, and Schukalla said, 'It wasn't really all that bad back in

Marzahn, was it? You got a slap every now and then, but no worse than that, eh?'

I'm not sure quite how it came about, but I was made a prefect at the camp school, along with my sister: I was the prefect for the boys, and she for the girls. Maybe it was because we worked hard and were keen to help others.

My sister Therese and I were very close. We were the youngest two siblings. Therese had a heart valve defect. When her heart wasn't beating as it should, her whole head would tremble – that's how bad it was. Back then, we were too poorly informed, I must admit, to take her to hospital. A doctor prescribed her some drops, but they didn't help. She was smarter than me, though, and much further ahead in reasoning and writing. I can only imagine how hard she must have found all the chores that she was expected to do as a girl: cleaning, washing up, sweeping out the wagons, and all the rest of it.

I was always the first one at school in the morning. I was allowed to ring the big bell that hung on a rope at the entrance. 'Ding, ding, ding!'

When they heard it, the children would emerge

Otto (centre) with his sister Therese
(to his left), Berlin-Marzahn camp, *c.*1936

from their huts or caravans. The cleaning lady had already done her rounds. Then the teacher would enter, walk to the front and greet us with 'Heil Hitler! Sit!' The first order of business was 'Hands on the table!' Anyone whose fingernails or hands were dirty had to go out and wash them clean, and only then were they allowed to come back in. After breaktime came the order 'Shoes off! Show me your feet!' Anyone who had dirty feet had to go and wash them. The whole thing was a bit of a laugh, though. If you were singled out, you had to go to the outside pump. One person would work the pump, while the others would wash and run about, splashing the water. Of course, that's just the sort of thing that children love.

If any pupils were absent, the teacher would say, 'Otto, go and tell them that they need to come to school.'

I would go and knock on the door of their hut or caravan. Sometimes, they were fast asleep and came to the door all dishevelled, with feathers from their bedding in their hair.

'Hey, you've got to get to school! The teacher's waiting!'

'Oh no, we slept in!'

They got ready quickly and hurried to school. The teacher, Herr Barwich, would give them a scolding but leave it at that.

I got on well with everyone, even the policemen, Chief Sergeant Politz and First Sergeant Bredel. Bredel was generally feared, but not by me. They all knew me. It was all 'Otto, come here and fetch some coal from the shed!' or 'Otto, fetch some water!' I never said no. At the end of the day, I might get something in return, as they liked me being around.

A foreman kept the whole place spick and span. He put numbers on the huts and caravans to make it easier to locate someone quickly. If anyone came by at night, he would write down their names so that he could report them to the police. There was a steady stream of visitors, who were escorted around the camp by the police stationed there. They wanted to inspect and talk about everything.

Before long, some nine hundred to a thousand

people were living at the Marzahn camp, Roma along with Sinti. The Sinti included many of my aunts, uncles and other relations, including my grandmother's sister and her sons. We were a massive family.

One of my grandmother's brothers was named Otto, just like me. One day, a package came for me from the Convent of Christ the King, containing toothpaste, a toothbrush and handkerchiefs. I waited in vain for the postman to bring it; my uncle had got there first.

'Morning! Do you have a parcel for Otto Rosenberg?'

'Yes, I delivered it right over there.'

I went to my great-uncle's and said, 'That's my parcel!'

'What are you on about, boy! It's got my name on it!'

'Yes, but take a look at what's in it!'

'Hmm, you might have a point . . .'

I reckon there were fifty or so of us, but that guess might well be on the low side. And boy, did we work. My Uncle Florian was still carrying heavy loads on construction sites. That meant that he was able to buy nice things, including a leather jacket – a prized item back in the day.

One of my relatives worked in a wax factory in Neukölln; another worked at Hasse und Frede, a stone mill; and another in a crate factory in Hohenschönhausen.

My brother Max, who had previously worked at the Kabarett der Komiker, a variety theatre in Berlin, was conscripted to work at a ball-bearing factory in Neu-Lichtenberg. He was also checked for physical fitness and assigned to Training Reserve II. But the authorities found out that he had a German girlfriend. This was *verboten* due to his 'impure blood',[7] and it landed him in the Neuengamme concentration camp. Towards the end of the war he was loaded onto a ship that was accidentally shelled by the Brits, who had mistaken it for a boat commandeered for high-level Nazis to make their escape. He tried to get to safety and was shot dead.

Only the older folk stayed in the camp; the children went to school. A sense of almost complete order prevailed – almost, but not quite. Everyone knew

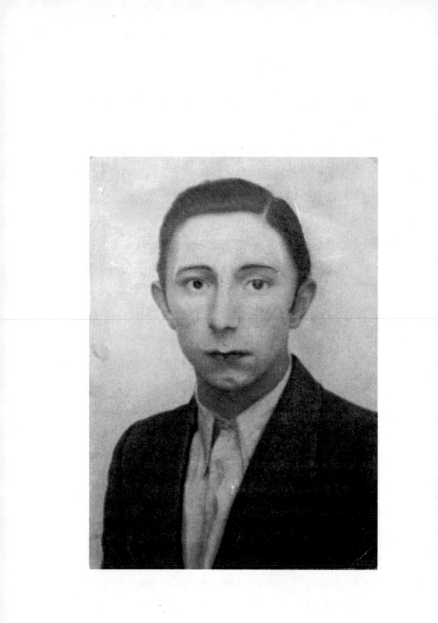

Max Rosenberg, *c.*1940

the whereabouts of everyone else. Everyone was registered. Those who could went out to work.

By Saturday or Sunday, the bread situation was dire – we had always run out by then. My grandmother had other children and grandchildren besides me, and they were no better off. They would come round asking for bread over the course of the week, and she'd give it to them. This infuriated me: 'They're picking us clean! Soon we won't have any left!' I used to weep and rage about it: 'I'm always hungry! Why is God punishing me like this?' Having nothing to eat often drove me to tears. My grandmother received no money save for her welfare support; it wasn't like we were out earning big bucks.

Luckily, I worked for the farmers on the other side of the railway tracks. They had apples, pears, plums, potatoes, and more besides – and I could take what I liked. I went in and out of the farmyard at my leisure, taking the cow to pasture and making everything neat and tidy. They weren't worried that I was going to steal something or abuse their trust.

'Otto, you can go pick cherries today.'

I picked five basketfuls, maybe more, and got to take one home for my trouble: 'Here, take these for your grandma.'

I helped other farmers harvest beets, too. If I dug up a row, I could earn 75 pfennigs, plus two buns dripping with icing. Sometimes we'd get less money in return, but plenty of food to make up for it. We couldn't have afforded milky coffee at home, for instance, so we were just happy to be well fed *and* able to bring 50 or 75 pfennigs back with us. That was a lot of money back then. A bread roll came to two or three pfennigs; a bun with a crumble topping was five. For three or four marks you could cook up a wonderful dinner for everyone.

The adults worked in the fields a lot, too. Some of the farmers' beet fields were so huge that if you started at the crack of dawn, you would only have got to the end of a row by nine or ten. Us kids couldn't have managed that, but the grown-ups would earn a mark for completing one of those long rows, which meant that they could sometimes make as much as six or seven marks by sundown. If you added in the pfennigs that the children earned, it might come to ten or even fifteen marks altogether. You could live off that for a whole week.

I was known all over the place by everyone, from Father Philipp to Herr Rohde, a wealthy farmer and local Nazi who used to drive around in a green Mercedes, even back then.

I often found myself sitting at the bus stop outside the big church in Marzahn, waiting for people I knew or seeing who might show up. While there, my gaze would sometimes drift over to the portal of the church and I'd start daydreaming of the tale of a magic coin that the old folk liked to tell.

To obtain this coin, you had to get a cat, put it in a sack and tie the sack closed with 99 knots. Then you'd go to the church before midnight and draw a chalk circle in front of the portal, stand inside it and wait for the clock to strike 12. Then you would brandish the sack and say, 'I have a lovely rabbit for sale.'

In an instant, the Devil would appear and say, 'I'd like to buy that rabbit.'

'All right then.'

'How much does the rabbit cost?'

'One taler.'

'One taler – is that all?'

'Yes, just one taler. I'll give you the rabbit, and you give me one taler.'

'It's a deal.'

You would give him the sack, and the Devil would start undoing the 99 knots. It would take him a while. At last, he would look in the sack and realize that you'd tricked him. In his fury, he would tear the cat to shreds and would have done the same to you, only he can't get at you because you're standing inside the chalk circle. He would then try all his wiles to lure you out, but you would stand your ground until the clock struck one.

'Bong, bong!' He would be gone in a flash. But not so fast – you'd need to sit down and stay in that circle until it started getting light. And then, on the ground, you'd spot a taler, but it wasn't just any old coin: you could spend it as often as you wanted, as it always ended up back in your pocket.

I was a firm believer in this tale as a child, so I'd often linger on the bus-stop bench outside Marzahn church, dreaming of the magic coin.

Speaking of buses, as Sinti, we weren't permitted

to sit on the padded seats on the lower deck of the bus; we had to go to the top, where there were only hard boards.

The threats became ever more menacing. We noticed a difference in the police; everything was now stricter and tougher.[8] If anyone had done something wrong or people got into a tiff or even a fight in the camp, the police turned on a massive searchlight and ran in with their sabres drawn. By that stage, they carried long sabres at their sides, not the shorter Wehrmacht-style ones. They were lit up by the dazzling searchlight, like something out of a film. Seen through a boy's eyes, it was all very cops and robbers, but when I think back on it, I also saw them beating people with their sabres – with the flat side, not the sharp edge. Then a riot squad would swoop in, grab the miscreants and whisk them away in their wagon.

In the early days, such disputes were easy to avoid, but that was no longer an option now. By this stage, Marzahn was home to people of all different origins and backgrounds. People from Hungary, Austria and Germany were living cheek by jowl, and that led to disagreements, usually sparked by the children.

The adults didn't usually get into arguments of their own accord; they knew that we were all in the same boat. But the children tended to get into scraps, one would get a nasty clip, one thing led to another, and before long the women were at each other's throats. The men would try to get between them and pull them apart, but that only made things worse and in no time half the camp was in uproar. Then Berlin's finest would roll in, restore calm and cart a load of people off to be locked up.

More and more people began vanishing, and we'd hear things about them getting a plot of land and settling farther east. Those were the kind of rumours that were going around the camp. Actually, I think we can call it a concentration camp at this point.

Our teacher, who by this stage taught us in uniform, too, showed us the positions of our German troops on a map, and where they were invading. We tracked all of it avidly.

The teacher started having a little tipple on the job. He would write a task on the board for us and then retire to his office. 'Otto, keep everyone in check and make sure they do their work!'

When the peasant who lived opposite the camp was drafted, the teacher befriended his wife. Their smallholding had only a single cow, named Minka, but presumably the woman was a good cook. One day, the teacher gave me a letter to deliver to the big high school in Marzahn, or so I thought. I dashed over there with it, but the school was a good 20 or 25 minutes away. When I returned, the teacher asked, 'How come you took so long? Did you hand over the letter?'

'Yes sir, I gave it to the Head.'

It was then I discovered that I was supposed to have given it to the peasant woman. I sprinted back to Marzahn.

'I'm sorry, sir, but that letter wasn't meant for you.'

'Yes, I noticed.'

The teacher was hopping mad, but there wasn't much he could do about it.

By now, there were frequent air-raid alarms. There were no bunkers for us at the camp, and if we happened to be in the city, the air-raid shelters there were off-limits to us, too. At Marzahn, we would leave our caravans and huts to watch the show. The kids were thrilled to see the searchlights of the anti-aircraft guns tracking the bombers. But we had to be careful – razor-sharp shrapnel from the air defences often whistled down into the camp. The next day, us youngsters would go out together to gather it all up.

There was an anti-aircraft emplacement close to the camp. I liked to visit the soldiers there: whenever I turned up, they'd say, 'Come here, Otto, what's the betting you're hungry?'

One time, they had cooked a lovely, thick split-pea stew. When I got home, my grandmother was asleep on the couch. I woke her with, 'Look, Mami, I've brought you a treat.'

Midway through eating, she suddenly remembered that it was a Catholic holy day of obligation.

'Oh no, Otto, I'm not supposed to eat anything today!'

'Too late now, Mami! Don't worry about it.'

To be honest, I really looked up to those soldiers, those big, blond-haired, blue-eyed men in their dapper uniforms.

At this point, people from outside could no longer come into the camp. The police assigned to us were stationed right outside. Morning after morning, they went to certain huts or caravans and took people away, never to be seen again. In ever-increasing numbers, people were ordered to report to Alexanderplatz, Dircksenstraße, Berlin C2, and Leo Karsten at the 'Gypsy Department'.[9] Karsten was the man in charge.

My mother, who by now was in Marzahn, was one of those sent to Dircksenstraße. She never came back to the camp. She went straight from Dircksenstraße to Ravensbrück.

I remember waiting at that bus stop outside the village church for her. The last bus that she could have returned on came and went, without her on it. It was so dark that I could hardly muster up the courage to make my way back home all alone. Somehow, I got back there in the end.

So many people were taken off like that, one by one.

Chapter Four

When I turned 13, I had to leave school. My grandmother was dependent on welfare and I was all grown up now, so it was up to me to support her.[10]

I went to the Labour Office, where I was issued with a booklet for time-stamping, a tax card and a disability-insurance card. I was conscripted to work in an armament factory in Berlin-Lichtenburg called Dannemann & Quandt Apparatebau. *Apparatebau* suggested a general engineering factory, but it actually manufactured shell casings for submarines.

I was popular with the foreman and my workmates in the factory paint shop. While there, I even managed to improve the dipping process. The usual thing was to dip just one ring into the paint at a time. You would pull a ring off an iron rod, hang it on a hook, dip it in, lift it back out, hang it up to dry, then put it back on the rod. It was all a bit too slow for my liking.

I said to Mr Levin – who I now think must have been Jewish – 'I need a long trough.' Levin was a man of many talents and really knew his way around the workshop. He welded and soldered away, and duly presented me with a long trough. I went to the foreman and said, 'I need a big vat of paint, not just a drop.' I poured the paint into the tub, then threaded several unpainted rings onto an iron rod, plunged them into the paint, took them out to dry and hung them up in the cart, ready for baking.

Before that, I had been getting 31 pfennigs an hour. Using the new dip-painting process made me another 4 pfennigs on top, upping my rate to 35 pfennigs per hour. You can imagine how good that felt; I was on top of the world.

My triumph was short-lived. One day, the foreman came over to me and said, 'Otto, I'm afraid you're being taken off manual work.'

'But why? This is where I belong, in the paint shop, and you know what I've done with the paints . . .'

'It's a no.'

My milk entitlement – everyone got given milk – was rescinded, too: orders from above.

'Why? What about the others?'

No milk for me, nor the small ration of meat that the men with a valid manual labour card received.[11]

Then – worst of all – I was barred from lunch in the canteen. Just imagine it. I hadn't done anyone any harm; I was very much still a kid. The staff breakfast my fellow workers tucked into first thing was now also off limits; I had to eat my bread at the woodpile out in the yard. I literally didn't have a place at the table.

I started to feel shunned. Plenty of people clearly felt bad about it, as they'd slip me some food and a kind word here and there. But many others didn't so much as bat an eyelid.

Herr Fischer, one of the factory stalwarts, a huge man with a curled goatee, packed up a lunch for me in some army cookware and put it on my woodpile, even though he wasn't supposed to.

'That's the best I can do, Otto.'

Then there was Herr Knop, who made up a

DAQUA

DANNEBERG & QUANDT

MASCHINENFABRIK · LUFT- U. WÄRMETECHNISCHE ANLAGEN

BERLIN-LICHTENBERG, SIEGFRIEDSTR. 202-204

GEGR. DAQUA 1879

Herrn

Otto Rosenberg

Berlin-Friedrichsfelde

Massower Str. 52

Ihre Zeichen	Ihre Nachr.	Unsere Z.	Tag
		Na.	23.5.49

BETRIFFT

Es ist uns bekannt, daß Sie in der Zeit von 1940 bis 1942 bei der Firma Danneberg & Quandt beschäftigt waren und Ihnen die Schwerarbeiterkarte nicht zugestanden wurde.

Danneberg & Quandt

Fernsprecher: 55 41 87 — Telegrammadresse: DAQUA Berlin — Postscheckkonto Berlin 122 99

(33) Berliner Druckhaus (2) I. P. J. Mi. V. 4406/44

Confirmation of the denial of supplementary food rations for manual workers, Berlin, 1949 package of children's things for Christmas. 'Here, boy, take this.'

They were exceptions, though: when all this started happening, lots of people stopped speaking to me and would blank me if I said hello. Perhaps more of them would have been nicer to me if they hadn't been afraid of the Gestapo and getting pegged as someone who was slipping things to the gypsy. That kind of thing might have got them in trouble.

The foreman, a man named Günther, wore a black uniform emblazoned with a swastika, but he wasn't SS himself. I'm not sure what the uniform was all about. One day, he called me over: 'Rosenberg!' It sounded urgent. I hurried into his office.

'Quick, take this, but stash it away so no one sees.' I found myself holding a jar of jam.

When he came by to check on my work later, anyone would have thought that he was a harsh taskmaster: 'Come on, move it, work that broom, no time to waste!' But appearances can be deceptive: he was all right. I looked him up again after 1945, by which time he had moved on to a different company. I said hello and thanked him for what he had done for me.

The journey to work was maybe the worst part of my day. I had to make a long detour to get around the police. This usually meant walking along the railway line towards Lichtenberg. The trains that stopped at Marzahn were made up of passenger carriages and freight wagons. Often, I'd jump onto one of the freight wagons and hide in the empty brakeman's cab. It was lovely in summer, but winter was a different matter altogether. If it was snowing and you decided to go the standard way, past the policemen, to catch the bus, chances are that it wouldn't come. Then you'd be left with no choice but to head to the station via the usual route; only now the train would already have left, with the next one only half an hour later. And if you walked along the tracks, you ran the risk of slipping off and sliding all the way down the steep embankment onto the alarmed wires. 'Ding, ding, ding, ding!'

The police let their dogs bite anyone they caught, and would dole out beatings of their own before bringing them in. Thank God it never happened to me.

All this could make me an hour or two late. Herr Kramer, the chief foreman – I actually saw him after

'45, too, but no sooner had he glanced my way than he was gone – would come by and say, 'Rosenberg, be late once more and, mark my words, it'll be off to the concentration camp with you.' Every single time. Being upbraided the umpteenth time for the same offence, always uttered in this offhand fashion – well, it all got a bit much for me one day, and I told him where to get off.

I was still a nipper, really. He should have tried putting himself in my shoes. Work began at seven, so I was getting up at half five, at the age of just fifteen. He'd lie in wait, just so that he could come down on me with, 'Well, well, Rosenberg! Late for work again. Do that once more and it's straight to the concert camp with you, you hear me?'

In spite of everything, I was always a keen little helper. I was happy to fetch lemonade, beer and cigarettes for all and sundry, and if anyone was away, I'd pick up their share of cigarettes and hand it on to someone else. I didn't smoke, after all, and it meant that I'd get something to eat in return.

The kiosk where I had to go to get things was in the munitions hall, where the finished submarine shell casings were stored. One fine day, I was walking through the hall when I spotted a 'burning glass'. This lens must have been used to check the canisters for defects and cracks, although that didn't occur to me at the time. Wow, I thought, it makes everything look massive!

I unfastened it and smuggled it away to the log pile – the one I ate lunch at – to burn some letters into the wood, messing around as boys like to do. But I must have been spotted. Along came another employee, a bloke named Siebert.

'Oi, Otto – Kramer the Chief Foreman saw what you did, unscrewing that lens and taking it off with you.' Actually, he may have called it a burning glass. One or the other.

In a momentary panic, I lifted up the paint kettle and shoved the thing underneath it.

'I didn't unscrew anything.'

'Oh yes you did,' he said. 'Don't be daft. Foreman Schmäler saw you, and so did Kramer. Hand it over. They'll screw it back on, and no harm done.'

'Fine,' I said. 'I wasn't trying to pinch it, though, I just wanted to . . .'

I handed over the piece of glass. They screwed it back on, and that seemed to be that.

It was four o'clock – home time. But as I made to leave the factory, the porter told me to come back in and sit down.

'Why?' I asked. 'What's the problem?'

'Just wait right there.'

After a little while, the door opened and a policeman came in.

'Is that him?'

'Yes,' said the porter. 'That's him.'

'Aren't you going to stand up?' he barked. I had no idea what was going on. He fastened a metal chain and a cord around my arm to restrain me, took me to the tram and escorted me to some police station or other. It was utterly humiliating; I was distraught.

At the police station, they filled out a report on the whole burning glass affair and arrested me. They wanted to lock me in a cell.

'Please don't lock me up! Leave the door open!'

So they left the door open but gave me a bucket and a rag. 'You're not going anywhere, so you might as well mop the floor.'

By the time I was done, it must have been six or seven in the evening. 'I've been at work since first thing this morning,' I said. 'I'm really hungry.' One of them had some bread and the other some leftover jam, which they gave me to eat. Then they went back to wanting to lock me in the cell. 'Please, I'm not going in there!' I said. 'If I have to, at least leave the door open!' I had never been in such a place before, which is why I was so scared. They left the door open.

The next morning, I was taken to Dircksenstraße. They brought me down to the basement, where the men were kept. Loud, rough men, some 30 or 40 of them. No beds, nowhere to sit, no space; just a little table and a swarm of cockroaches. They shoved me in there and slammed the door, job done. 'Oh my God,' I said to myself, 'where on earth have you ended up now?'

There was no toilet in there either, just a curtain with some buckets behind it. And the stench – hell on earth. What was I supposed to do? There was nothing to sleep on. I crawled under the table and pulled my coat – which I still had with me – over my head. I fell asleep like that.

The next day the door flew open, and I heard, 'Otto Rosenberg!'

'Here!' Thank God, I thought. Free at last!

But no: I was handcuffed and put on a transport to Moabit Prison, Berlin 12A. In through the gate, jump down from the van and straight inside. I was held in a cell at first, before being called forward. They let me keep the clothes I had on, but everything else was taken away, including my papers. I was just a boy, so my possessions didn't amount to much – a couple of trouser buttons and a few pfennigs from my pockets.

Then it was off to the warden, who gave me some chequered bedding, a cover for my bolster pillow, and other such items. That done, I was escorted upstairs: 'F5, new inmate!' What a thing to hear! Can you imagine? How old would I have been back then – 15 or so, I think. I was taken to cell number 538. When the door slammed shut, it felt as though my whole world was crumbling in upon me. I stood there alone in my cell.

About half an hour later, I had to come out again for a shower. They put a gadget against my scalp and shaved my head. After showering, I was given some prison trousers, a jacket and a scarf. I was allowed to keep my coat and shoes. I felt a bit cleaner now, so in a sense I was glad to be out of Dircksenstraße. At that point, I still had no real idea what was going on.

I spent four months in solitary confinement in that cell, without being sentenced or anything.

We had to wear our prison scarves at all times, all the better to choke us with. You had to loop it round your neck in a certain way and then pull the end through. One time, the officer in charge reached into the gap between my neck and scarf and throttled me. My offence? To ask someone if they'd got some sausage, as I'd missed out. The prison dogsbodies often failed to serve up part of our meals.

Everything was subject to strict rules. When the guard opened the cell door for me the first time, I was standing in the middle of the cell, as you might expect.

'Why aren't you standing by the window?! Get over there right now! Hands where I can see them and report!'

How could I possibly have known the protocol? If the door was unlocked, you had to go over to the window right away, but no one had told me. 'What am I supposed to report?' I asked.

So he told me what to say: 'Cell 538, occupied by a pre-trial detainee. Nothing to report.' That was it.

Camba, my young aunt, came to visit me and brought me a pair of shoes. It was from her I learned that most of our family had been removed from Marzahn.[12]

At long last, I received a date for my hearing. I was assigned a lawyer, too, but he was really acting for the court, not me, and was probably a Nazi. I was sentenced to three months and three weeks in youth detention for sabotage – that's right – and theft of Wehrmacht property. By that time, though, I had already been there for four months. My sentence had been served, so out I came.

I didn't get far. No sooner had I left the gates than a policeman – not one of the prison staff – confronted me.

'You're under arrest.'

'Why? I've just been released from jail! I'm free!'

'Surveillance.'

So I was taken back to Dircksenstraße, but this time the Gypsy Department, where Karsten, whom I mentioned earlier, ruled the roost. Sitting alongside him was a Sinti man who lived in a caravan in Marzahn with his family and reported everything back to Karsten.

'Four months?' Karsten said. 'That's a nice long time.'

'So, how was it?' sneered the Sinti man. '*Was* it nice?'

'Yes, very nice,' I replied. I wasn't sure what else to say.

Karsten turned to the man. 'Well then, what shall we do with him?' And to me, 'Whatever are we to do with you? Where should we put you now?'

'With my aunt,' I said. I knew that there was almost no one left in Marzahn.

The Sinti man said, 'He'll go where his mother and father have gone.' I didn't know what that meant, but I was happy to hear it.

After the war, some Sinti people handed this informant over to the Russians. The Russians said, 'Just kill him if you want. Go ahead – there won't be any repercussions.' But they didn't kill him. Instead, a Sinti woman slapped him around the head – one of our biggest insults – and the traitor was taken off to Siberia.

First, I was sent down to the vaulted cellar, where three families with little children were already waiting. I was pleased to see them, having been alone for so long. Another girl came in later. The others joked, 'She can't sleep with us – she'll have to sleep with you.' But it wasn't like that; we slept top and tail.

Conditions were awful there, too – there weren't any proper toilets or anything, so it was pretty dire. We were held there for a few weeks before the transport came. At that point, I was separated from those families. I'm not sure where the train left from.

I was still classed as a prison inmate, so I was put in a special carriage. There were only children in there, all nicely dressed and carrying their lunchboxes and satchels. I guess they could have been Sinti or Roma kids, but they didn't all look like it. They came from Catholic children's homes. Cute little faces. They were all about six to eight years old, a carriage full of them.

The police put me in a cell by the door into the carriage and locked me in there. Thankfully, it had a seat. The police left, and the military took over the transport, as far as I know. The guard sat there stolidly with his automatic rifle, making sure no one came near me.

Once the train had been going for a while, the children began to ask the Red Cross sister who was accompanying them why I was locked up. She took it upon herself to petition the guard: 'Can't you let the boy out? It's not like he can go anywhere, is it?'

He relented and let me go and sit with the children. They all had full lunchboxes and sandwich bags. 'I'm starving,' I said, 'I haven't eaten a thing', so they gave me some of their food.

I arrived in Auschwitz on that train just before I turned 16. My mother and father were not there.

Chapter Five

We were taken to Groß-Auschwitz, the big main camp that you came to first. The train was made up of several transports coupled together, so we were sorted there right away: Sinti here, Jews there, Poles over here. Everyone was put into groups. We were assigned to a doctor, who would give a signal, usually ringing a bell and waving his arm: you go this way, you that way. His list was very long.

It was a well-oiled operation. All of a sudden, the children were nowhere to be seen and I was surrounded by young people about the same age as me. We had to roll up our sleeves and a Pole named Bogdan tattooed a number onto our arms with a kind of fountain pen. I was Z 6084.[13]

At first, I was assigned to the main camp and attended bricklaying classes. I already knew some of the lads who were working there from Marzahn. We carted sand around in wheelbarrows and learned how to mix mortar, use a trowel, lay bricks and position the bucket, all in a few quick moves. I've been able to lay bricks ever since.[14]

I don't know why, but after a month or so – or maybe it was just a few days – someone decided to put me somewhere else. 'Everyone line up! You, you and you.' I and a few others were taken over to the gypsy camp, as they called it, in Birkenau.[15] We marched as a group, always in single file, running occasionally then falling back into line. There was a constant refrain of 'Get over here! Step to it! Come here, you!'

We were rushed through the camp and allocated to different blocks. I started off in Block 3. Each block was an army-style barrack building, converted from stables.[16] These blocks, all 23 of them – or perhaps it was 26 – were arranged in two rows. Each was about ten metres long, perhaps a little longer, and four or five metres wide. The entire gypsy camp covered an area roughly 100 metres wide by 150 metres long.

The blocks contained wooden box beds stacked together in triple bunks. Every bunk was home to a family or a random assortment of people. The mattresses were sacks stuffed with shredded paper and wood shavings. The Jewish inmates had brought in longhair blankets that we used to cover ourselves. In the centre of the block was a large brick stove that was only built after I had arrived. It gave off heat on two sides, but it was never enough to warm up those huts in winter.

I had to report to the block elder. Later, during my free hour – the blocks were locked down before that, so no one could leave their hut – I asked around to find out if anyone else I knew was still there. My enquiries came to nothing, but a couple of days later I found out that my grandmother, my sister Therese, my cousins, aunts and uncles, and my half-brothers and half-sisters from my mother's second marriage were all at the camp.[17]

My uncles had all been in the military – cavalry, navy and infantry. One cousin was even in the Luftwaffe. Another had fought in Finland as part of the mountain troops. When he was on leave, he tried to visit my grandmother in Marzahn. At the police station, he was told, 'Your mother's in the concert camp. They've given people plots of land there, you know. They can build little houses and keep animals and all.'

My uncle said, 'I'm not fighting for a country that does this.' So they confiscated his gun, and 14 days later he ended up in Auschwitz, too.[18]

The elder for Block 3 was an ethnic German named Erich – a good guy. I was with him for quite a while.

When I was allowed out of the block, I went and found my grandmother. I managed to get over to her block as quickly as I could, with a bit of luck and help from others.

'Oh, my darling boy!'

My Uncle Florian – the one who used to work on building sites – was a block clerk at the camp. He maintained records of everyone who was in the block, kept tabs on food supplies, and so on.

I was assigned to work under Block Elder Hans Koch, a man from Cologne. After the war, I saw him right here in Berlin, standing at the Sonnenallee S-Bahn station.

'Hey, you're Hans Koch!'

'Oh . . . no, no, that's not me. I'm Hans Walter Kaiser!' But I recognized him all right. He dodged me, ran through the barriers and was gone. He used to beat me up in the concentration camp, you see. All those years later, though, I was just glad to be free; I wouldn't have done anything to him.

I worked alongside Günter, a man from Hamburg whom I also knew from Marzahn. He's dead now. We kept everything clean and tidy and kept the store running. The SS had a kind of room in his block and were always taking women in there in the evenings. The block elder was involved, too. They'd drink and make a mess, and we were expected to clean it up. They left their filth there, disgusting things. Dealing with it was against my laws. I said, 'No way, I'm not doing that!' The block elder beat me with his cudgel, threw me out and reported me for refusing to work.

I wasn't aware yet that making a stand like that could have such terrible consequences. What's more, as a newcomer to Auschwitz, I had no idea that a block elder, who seemed to be a mere go-between, could have so much power. But I soon found out.

Most of the block elders were ethnic Germans and almost always hardened criminals who had been taken to the camp from prisons and penitentiaries. They essentially did the bidding of the SS within the camp.

The hierarchy among the inmates worked like this: first there was the camp elder, then his deputy, with the clerks in the office under him. Then came the block elder, the block clerk, the room leader and the gatekeeper. Of course, all of them were subordinate to the SS, the camp commander and his deputy. The block elder was subordinate to the block leader, who was also SS.

If anyone screwed up in the block, the punishment was meted out to the block elder along with everyone else. The inmates would have to crawl along the ground in pairs, say, with the block leader or another SS man pressing a foot into their backs. If they didn't go fast enough, out came the whip. Then they'd have to get up and run. 'On your feet! Now march! Lie down! Do squats! Jump!' Of course, this would send the block elder into a rage, and when he made it back to the block, he'd lash out.

'If anyone in this block so much as puts a foot out of line, I'll beat the living daylights out of the lot of you!'

Everyone trembled. Sometimes the block elder was just in a bad mood, and you only had to walk past him to set him off. 'Oi, you! Get over here!'

It's worth pointing out that the camp elders – and the block elders, too, come to think of it – had a cushier life in the camp than they would have done elsewhere. They could get anything they wanted, even wine or women.

There was a strict chain of command. For work crews, the chief kapo was at the top, followed by the kapo, then the deputy kapo and the supervisors – all inmates tasked with making sure that the work got done.[19] They all had their own specific duties but also enjoyed a level of authority that they would wield to different degrees. They could beat people up or get along famously with them; it was entirely up to the individual. Some of them could be erratic and treated people according to how they happened to be feeling at the time. If roll call hadn't gone as smoothly as they would have liked, for instance, they might turf the entire block out and make us stand there for hours on end – men, women and children. Roll calls were always fraught with risk.

As a newcomer, I hadn't yet grasped the way the camp and its hierarchy worked. I wasn't aware of the status enjoyed by the block elder, either. He was unimaginably powerful, holding sway over life and death itself.

Before long, I was punished for supposedly refusing to work. As I recall, I had to wear a jacket with a red dot on the back and was made to march from the gypsy camp to the Jewish camp.[20]

The Jewish camp was a prison camp for men only. Everything there had to be done at a run; there was no standing still, even for a moment. There was a constant refrain of 'Keep it up! Keep it up!' If they caught you standing still, you'd get an instant beating. You had to be constantly on the move – 'Run! Let's go! Move it!' I was a young lad back then, but the older men who couldn't keep up didn't last long.

There were plenty of harsh measures in the gypsy camp, too, but everything was a whole lot worse in the main camp. Whenever you heard, 'Everybody out!' it was time to run for your life. If anyone turned up late in the morning, they'd get a beating. Some inmates worked sluggishly and attracted the supervisors' wrath, so they were always getting hit. Maybe they were ill, but no one bothered to find out – 'Lazy dog. We'll teach you.'

We lugged sand and rocks here and there with just a shovel – there were no wheelbarrows – and always in a triangle formation. Some of it was just work for the sake of it, but we also unloaded wagons of cement and stones. A sack of cement was hoisted onto every man's shoulders, and if you didn't get moving fast enough, they'd pile another on top of you, so you'd end up staggering around with a weight of a hundred kilos or more. My legs almost broke under the strain.

We converted old stables into dormitory huts, too. That meant digging out the soil and bringing in sand in big wooden caddies, which were heavy in their own right. Gravel went down on top of the sand, followed by boards and clay. We built the bunk boxes, too.

The Jewish camp was right next to the gypsy camp. One day, I was over by the electric fence when I saw my grandmother on the other side. She called out, 'Come over to the fence tonight!'

I went there that evening, and she threw me a wrapped loaf of bread. At the time, I presumed that it must have come from my Uncle Florian, the block clerk, but when I was back with her again, I found out that it was her own bread. I quarrelled with him because of it: 'You can get bread for sandwiches any time you like! I can't believe you're making Mami throw over her own bread!'

One time, a block elder in the gypsy camp asked my uncle to make up a huge parcel of bread and throw it over the fence to someone else. The person didn't show up, but I was there, so he tossed it to me. What a feast that was!

On another occasion, a block leader on my side saw my grandmother throwing something over the fence to me. She kept her head down and hurried away. The block leader hit me, not on my behind or my back, but right in between, where it really hurt. Every blow knocked me to the floor. 'Get up!' he shouted. Again and again, he hit me. It was strictly forbidden to have conversations through the wire fence. But all through my beating I just thought to myself, that bread will save my life.

At one point, I fell ill and collapsed. Some Sinti who knew me took me to the infirmary with the paramedic. Some said it was typhus; others spotted fever or malaria. I'm still not sure what was actually wrong with me.

The block elder for the infirmary was named Ernst Rosin – I remember that very clearly. He was a nice man, too. The world is full of terrible people, but there are always a few good eggs among them.

The sick barracks in the Jewish camp were small, low-slung masonry buildings, rather than wooden huts, but they had the same old wooden bunk boxes.

My senses started to fade away. Sweat was pouring out of me and I was struggling to breathe. I drifted in and out of consciousness, my mouth chapped from fever. Occasionally, someone would come over and feed me a spoonful of white paste. 'Okay, go back to sleep.'

You either recovered or you didn't; no one cared which it was. In the bunk next to me lay a

Dutchman – or maybe he was Belgian – who received a lot of parcels. The third bunk was now empty; the man who had been in there had died, so there were just the two of us left. My neighbour started croaking incessantly, 'Water! Water!'

I knew that he had a parcel but that he didn't want to share. 'Give me something from that,' I said, 'and I'll go fetch you some water.'

Drinking water was actually forbidden; we were only allowed to drink tea. Anyone caught fetching or drinking water was beaten to death, as the water was contaminated with typhoid. The idea was to stop typhoid fever from spreading.

I had a red cup that I could tie onto my clothing. With it hidden under my prison coat, I crept out of my bunk and over to the washroom. The water was turned off, but I knew how to get some out nonetheless. You just had to turn on the tap and suck on it, then block the outflow with your tongue as soon as you felt the water. Then you could pop the cup underneath, and a little water would always come out. I spat the water from my mouth into the cup, too. When it was half full, I carried it slowly back to my bunk, climbed up, put the cup down and gave my bunkmate a shake: 'Hey, I got your water for you!'

He was dead. Just lying there, dead. Oh, dear God, I thought. And the very next instant: now I can take his parcel.

I had to make sure that the room leader, who sometimes looked in on us, wouldn't notice anything. I carefully prised the parcel out from underneath the body and took out all the things I needed, one by one, until there was hardly any food left in there. I stashed my newly acquired provisions under my pillow but left the parcel where it was. Then I called out to the room leader, 'Stubowi! Stubowi! A man's died!' At that time, the Poles did this job.

'Chuck him out,' he said.

Chuck him out? Not a chance – I tried lifting him, but he wouldn't budge. I manoeuvred him with my feet instead, inching him towards the edge, little by little, until I could finally shove him out. He crashed down onto the floor. They grabbed him by the legs and dragged him away, his head bouncing thud-thud-thud on the ground as he went.

The parcel gave me the boost I needed. I was

feeling better within a week and was able to leave the infirmary and resume working outside the camp.

In the mornings, we were woken by a guard banging on a piece of iron that hung outside the block. It sounded a bit like a triangle. We marched out of the camp and set to work levelling the earth. There were no wire fences here, only guards. We cleared away old debris – cardboard, that sort of thing – and burned all manner of stuff.

Once, when we were working out there, a lad ventured a little too near the cordon of guards and some blockhead shot him. That's just how it went sometimes. Afterwards, we laid him on an old door and carried him back into the camp. The story was that he had tried to flee, but all he had wanted was to pick some slender little sorrel leaves. I liked to eat them, too. You could gather a few, roll them up and pop them in your mouth for a little flavour.

We had to wear a cap with our prison uniforms, and whenever an SS officer went by, no matter who it was, you had to whip it off your head right away, put your hands down by your sides and march, looking him in the eye, declare your number and report anything that was going on. If there was nothing to report, you just had to march on past. Those guards would look at inmates' numbers, and if one of them made a note of yours, you knew your time was up.

After a while, I came to a decision. I reported to my overseers. 'Z 6084 would like to go to the office!'

There I met none other than Camp Commander Schwarzhuber, a lean, wiry man.[21]

'Z 6084 reporting, sir! I would like to make a request!'

I told him that I was from Berlin, that my grandmother was over in the gypsy camp, and that I wanted to be over there with her.

'What's this?' he said in his thick Bavarian accent. 'Your German is very good!'

'Yes, I'm from Berlin.'

I was a bundle of nerves. He looked me up and down and asked a few questions, all of which I answered.

'Hmm,' he said, 'if I find out that you're telling lies, we'll be having words.'

'*Jawohl!*'

There I stood before Schwarzhuber. If he could

verify what I'd said, I would be allowed to go over, but I must admit, I wasn't all that hopeful. In the morning, I suddenly heard my number called out: 'Z 6084 to the office!'

I honestly thought, 'That's it, I've had it.'

'Your request has been approved. You can go over.'

I let out a sigh of relief. Schwarzhuber wasn't even there.

There were a few of us being transferred together. ''Ten-shun! March in time!' We had to march over there like soldiers. How happy I was, and how utterly relieved to be back with my grandma again. Plus, I thought to myself, I'd be able to get a bit more food now – surely that could be arranged.

Chapter Six

I was given the role of gatekeeper in my grandmother's block. Before he appointed me, Wally the block elder dealt me five blows with his cosh, saying, 'There's more where that came from if you let anyone out of here without my say-so. No one leaves during block curfew.'

Anyone who wasn't working had to stay in their block all day. That included the elderly folk, who looked after the children instead of working. They had one free hour a day, when they could go for a walk along the street that ran through the camp or scurry off somewhere to pay someone a visit.

You also had to use that time to go to the toilet, in a hut with a latrine running down the middle, and a concrete panel with spaced-out holes on top. People had to do their business sitting opposite or alongside one another, and most people were ill at any given time. It was horrendous. The women would cover their faces with a cloth, but it didn't take away from the horror of the place, which broke all my people's greatest taboos. It bore no resemblance to the normal practice of relieving yourself; it was pure torment and debasement.

All our hair was shaved off, including our pubic hair and any growing under our arms. They used the same scissors for those areas as they did for our scalp and any facial hair. It's still hard for me to talk about such things.

Later, when I was working in the sauna, I saw my grandmother there, holding the little ones against her, and I turned around quickly. I knew she would be mortified if her grandson saw her like that. There can be no greater humiliation than forcing women to go naked in front of their grown-up sons, or men before their daughters.

A gong sounded to mark the end of our free hour, and everyone was supposed to be back at barracks by that time. Those who weren't already inside and turned up late or were caught on the main street by the block leaders were harshly punished.

'Where are you from? Which block?'

Some were shot on the spot, while others were taken into their block, laid over the tile stove and beaten or whipped.

My gatekeeping duties all went fairly smoothly, until one day a woman came to me with her child and said she urgently needed to take him to the toilet.

'No,' I said, 'I can't let anyone out.'

Her husband came along and started kicking up a fuss. What can I say: I'm a human being and when someone starts pleading with me, I respond, even if I know deep down that there might be consequences. Eventually I relented: 'All right, all right, but please be careful! And if they catch you, don't tell them that I let you out!'

Guess what happened? That's right – they got caught.

'Where have you come from?'

Then the SS officer and the block elder came at me and gave me twenty blows or more with a stick.

I was supposed to count along, but I couldn't keep up as those blows rained down between my hips and lower back. It was indescribably painful to lie down, sit or stand afterwards.

I kept my post as gatekeeper, but I never let anyone out again. And wouldn't you know it, the woman's husband blamed me for the incident. She had received her own beating from the block elder. I think her child may have been beaten, too, but I'm not sure.

'No,' I retorted, 'it's your fault – you told me to let you out!'

The man grabbed a hooked knife and went for me. Luckily, my cousin Oskar stepped between us, brandishing his cudgel, and beat him back. Wally, the block elder, came in at that very moment.

'What's going on, Oskar?'

Oskar told him what had happened. The block elder gave the man such a beating that he left me in peace from then on.

Oskar wielded a certain amount of control in our block. I must admit, he wasn't terribly kind to the people there; in fact, he was very tough on them. If he happened to be in the yard and saw someone make a wrong move, he would be right over there to hit them. Had Oskar survived Auschwitz, I'm certain that some people would have tracked him down and killed him. But he was my cousin, after all, and I didn't want to see him dead. I survived Auschwitz and know that I can look anyone from there straight in the eye. I never did anyone any harm. I'm just content to have got out of there.

Of course, I now had a cudgel of my own. There were times when a few people dived right into the food bucket to get out any leftovers, and I may have swung it at them.

'Get lost!'

That made them scram and gave me the chance to fill my own cup. But then I had to make myself scarce, as I knew they'd be coming back for me. I can chuckle about it now, but back then it was all deadly serious.

The people working in the kitchen used to steal a few potatoes and put them in a pot. When the block elder wasn't around, I would take the cover off the barrack stove – this was long and ran right the way through the hut, with a vent at each end – shove the pot in there, and close it up again. If the block elder had caught me, he would have hanged me for sure. But once the potatoes were cooked, I got to take some of them for myself. That was the sort of thing I got up to as a gatekeeper. It all helped me get by.

Those who were low down in the pecking order and didn't have anyone to help them would invariably die. If you got beaten, you were a marked man. The weak and emaciated, with death staring out of their sunken faces, aroused such aggression in their overseers that they were beaten all the more, until one day they dropped dead. Inmates like that didn't stand a chance. Only those who managed not to get sick and stayed strong enough to work had any prospect of survival. The slogan was 'Work makes you free', which turned into 'Extermination through labour', and that's no exaggeration. People were forced to work themselves until their bodies had nothing left to give.

The food was awful. In the morning, the room orderly would give us tea from a kettle and a quarter of a small loaf. And we were cheated even of those meagre rations: when the loaf was cut into quarters, they took a thick slice out of the middle, which became the children's bread ration. There was hardly ever any proper lunch, either, just stinging nettles and bits of cabbage floating in dishwater-like slop. You couldn't possibly nourish yourself on that.

As far as I remember, I lost my job as a gatekeeper when we were moved to a different block. I ended up working for a Pole. He was a big man named Jurek, and he spent the entire day drunk. How he managed that, I have no idea. He always had cigarettes, drink and food from the kitchen. And what food it was – meat included! When he was out, I would pilfer some of his stash. One time, he realized that his food was a bit short. He beat me up and booted me out, but that didn't put me off. I'd been beaten up so many times that it no longer acted as a deterrent.

I got sick again. This time I was covered in scabies from head to foot. There was no way I could work; I couldn't even bear to bring my fingers together, what with the itchy spots and pus. It was awful.

I was treated with Mitigal, a white, milky liquid, which was hideous, too, but it made the infestation clear up eventually.

I keep coming back to a single question: why did I survive? And I simply don't have the answer. Out of my whole family, including all my siblings and everyone dear to me, not a single one stood a chance of survival. And that's in spite of the fact that my brothers were much bigger and stronger than me – I was the smallest of the lot! I can't get my head around it. People say to me, 'Hey, at least you're free now – you should be glad!' But all I can think about is my brothers and sisters, and how they were taken, and even now it's hard to find joy in this world. On festive occasions, when people gather to celebrate and families meet up, I've often retreated into myself, into my pain. It's very hard.

When Hans Koch was my block elder, I got to know a woman named Sonja. She's still alive today. I've had a couple of visits from her son, too – we played cards. Sonja was a block clerk for Koch. I got on well with her; neither of us gave the other any trouble.

'What's up, little man?' she asked. Everyone called me that because I was so small.

'Nothing. Koch kicked me out, remember? He beat me up and got me sent to the work camp. Well, the camp commander let me come back here, thank God. But now I'm in the doghouse again.'

'Oh dear. You know what, I'll ask Kapo Felix. Maybe he can find a use for you.'

Kapo Felix was in a relationship with her sister, who acted as his clerk. She was as good as her word, and Felix gave me the task of running the sauna.

The sauna was a barrack hut in the gypsy camp that was made up of a disinfection station, bathing facilities and the sauna itself.[22] The sauna had nothing to do with losing weight – we were all scrawny enough as it was – but was there to cleanse. It had showers – real ones, not gas. I got into a good routine there and felt as though I'd found my feet again.

Everything ran like clockwork under Kapo Felix. I would get up in the morning, leave my block, go to my place of work, do my duties and return to my block once I'd finished. I worked for him right through until July 1944, when I was transferred to Buchenwald.

Unfortunately, I don't know what became of him. He was a strong, burly man, but I never once saw him beat or berate anyone. I think he must have been a political prisoner.[23]

I delivered reports and fetched things for him, including lunch, tea and coffee. All that toing and froing meant that I had the opportunity to help my three half-brothers and two half-sisters from my mother's second marriage. When I went to pick up food, I always walked past the block where they were staying. Snatching a moment together wasn't usually possible: I was always working, and by the time I'd finished for the day, it was block curfew. But after a while, I thought I'd better give it a try anyway. I went out with a pot to fetch food for the kapo, but instead of going straight back to him, I headed to the block where my half-siblings were, poured some into their bowls and then returned to the kitchen.

'The kapo would like some more.'

They gave me a second helping, no questions asked. And now that it had worked once, I did it again and again. But it was all just a drop in the ocean. My brothers and sisters were already doomed, and there was nothing I could have done to prevent it. The wailing that broke out whenever I came in and they saw me! If only I could have taken them out of there with me. It could never have happened, though – you couldn't help anyone openly, only on the sly.

When I mention my siblings in this block, I'm talking about my eldest sister, who was my father's daughter from his first marriage, my own sister Therese, who grew up with me at my grandmother's, and the five children that my mother had with her second husband. The eldest of them, Harry, was about ten. The children were tattooed, too, on the thigh. I only met my eldest half-sister, Drosla – the one who stayed with my father when I went to Berlin – when I arrived in Birkenau. By then, she was married with several children; I think her surname was Dembrowski.[24]

We realized that we were siblings completely by chance, through talking to other people. I happened to mention my parents, word got back to her, and she came up and hugged me.

'Come here, love – I hear you're my brother!'

She stayed in Auschwitz with her husband and all

Otto's half-sisters from his mother's second marriage –
Reibkuchen, Buchela and Traubela

of their children, and none of them made it out alive. I was glad to have met her, of course, but ultimately, I couldn't do anything to help her. We were all in a state of abject misery, and everyone had to do what they were told on pain of death. We did manage to see each other from time to time and chat about my father.

I have no idea how I managed to survive Auschwitz. To this day, I still can't fathom it. There was certainly a great deal of luck involved, but I believe there was something else, too – a protective hand held over me, shielding me from harm.

The camp overseers had a policy of tearing families apart by splitting them up. The upshot was that people would only care for themselves; there could be no more compassion, no putting others first. By the end, the father would readily eat his own child's bread.

In a concentration camp that wasn't designated a family camp, everyone hoarded what they were given because they knew it was their only chance of survival. In the camp, a piece of bread or a potato was infinitely more valuable than a 1,000-mark note – you can't eat the latter, after all. Before long, you knew to depend on every little scrap that came your way. And if you spotted a chance to snatch something extra, you simply had to summon up your courage and go for it. I got lots of beatings that way, but I'd already factored them in when I went to the kitchen and grabbed this or that – potato peelings, perhaps, or later, in Ellrich, scraps of food that the Wehrmacht had thrown away. I just shoved them into my cap and ran. If I got caught, they wrote down my number, which meant either a thrashing straight away, or my number getting called out for a punishment later. But I didn't care; all I could think about was getting something to eat.

My sister Therese never left Auschwitz, either, but she didn't die in the gas chambers; it was her heart valve defect that killed her. She was cremated like the rest.

One time, I went to the crematorium with Kapo Felix and saw it for myself, although I wasn't supposed to be looking around, but helping to carry the round canisters containing Zyklon B. To get there, we had to go out of the gypsy camp, accompanied by SS guards, of course. We did it in two or three trips.

'Come along,' he said.

I didn't see the gas showers, but I did notice the

ovens and the carts that were used to transport the bodies to the fires.

We took the canisters and returned to our camp. There I held a kind of toothed chisel against the middle of a canister and hit it with a hammer. This would break off a piece of the casing, and you could take out these little square grains, coloured turquoise or blue. A few of these were enough to delouse a whole heap of blankets and clothing.

We were all subjected to this delousing process, block by block, men and women.[25] Actually, as far as I remember the men went first, followed by the women. Come to think of it, men and women may only have been separated later, when Kapo Felix took charge of the procedure.

At any rate, first they had to walk through a basin containing a solution that killed bacteria and fungi. Once they were inside the showering area, Kapo Felix turned on the water and everyone washed themselves. Meanwhile, their clothing was hung up on trolleys and taken away to be deloused, which meant passing it through a vapour bath. The inmates would collect them on the other side and put them back on. This was done block by block, and once the final block was finished, it would start all over again from the beginning.

I'd never seen anything like it. The lice were absolutely everywhere, in countless numbers. It wasn't a matter of scraping them into a pile by hand; you needed a shovel. Heaps of them came out in each and every delousing. If you shook a blanket, they would scatter everywhere like grains of sand. The place was teeming with them.

The sauna had been built to get on top of the situation. The camp leaders, work managers, block leaders – all SS – came here, too, and went through the process themselves. While they were showering, I had to clean their shoes or boots. They came out to find them sparkling clean. Fine and dandy. It wasn't a bad job, all things considered.

The Kanada Kommando came to the sauna, too.[26] These people were tasked with taking people to the gas chambers to be killed and then cremating them in the ovens. They were rotated every six weeks, either because they couldn't bear to do it any longer or because knowledge of what was going on couldn't be allowed to leak out.

When the Jews arrived at Auschwitz, they didn't go straight into the camp. They were gathered on the tracks on the other side of our fence at Birkenau. There the families were sorted into mothers with children, young people and older people. They had to leave all of their suitcases and other belongings where they were. They were told that they would be taken off to shower, but most of them went straight to the gas chambers and were cremated immediately afterwards. They had no idea what was happening to them. They believed they were just going off to shower, but that stuff, the Zyklon B, was thrown in from above and then the water was turned on. When combined with the water, the chemical created a gas that killed them all.

We knew what was going on in there. Everyone did. One time, a committee came round the camp and asked the children what the ovens and chimneys back there were for – the crematoria were just a few hundred metres away. 'For baking bread,' the children replied. They were scared of being killed if they told the truth, you see.[27]

Any newcomers who were fit to work were allocated to camps where other inmates had died or more workers were needed.

The Kanada Kommando wrenched out the teeth of the new arrivals, pulled off their rings and snatched other items. I don't know what other terrible kinds of things they did to people.

They worked closely with the SS. Some of the Jews brought gold, diamonds and money to the camp with them, not to mention the finest soaps, fragrances, lipsticks and so on. When the Kanada Kommando came to the sauna to shower and delouse, I would take their clothes and hang them in the cart for disinfection. Of course, I always rummaged through their pockets to see what I could find. I knew that when the Kommando members came out the other side of the sauna, our paths would not cross again. There would have been no comeback even if I had nicked everything they had on them, but I just took little bits and bobs that I might be able to use or swap, like biscuits. Besides, if you bit into one of those biscuits, you might well find a little ring or part of a necklace. The Jews often baked such treasures into their provisions.

The people from the Kanada Kommando got the best food, lived lavishly and slept soundly in their beds. But when their six weeks were up, they too were sent to the gas chambers. I'm not sure whether they were aware of what would happen to them, but that's what Kapo Felix told me.

He was an ethnic German, so, although he was one of the inmates, he wasn't classed as an enemy of the Third Reich, as we were. We no longer had the right to call ourselves Germans. Ethnic Germans like Felix had a lot of say in what went on; in some cases, they were actually in cahoots with the SS and ran scams. The Kanada Kommando were knee deep in it. All sorts of things came into the camp – gold, money, you name it. The finest furs were taken off Jews and given to the wives of SS officials to wear.

Camp commanders, work managers, the lot – they all came to the sauna. One of the work managers who used to come had a limp. He was a big man who walked with a cane. The children would always run up behind him, trying to get close enough to touch him, in a sort of dare.

Dr Mengele came to the sauna to shower, too. Whenever word got around that Dr Mengele was in the camp, the children would run to meet him. He would take them by the hand and walk them round behind the sauna, where the infirmary lay.

His driver – when he used one and didn't drive himself, that is – arrived in an open-topped jeep. You could see all sorts of jars nestled on the shelf at the back: big, small, tall and short. They were filled with various substances, but I couldn't say what.

When he reached the door of the infirmary, Dr Mengele always put his white coat on before going inside.

I visited the infirmary for myself once. Some of the people in there had an incision in their skin above or below the knee, with another cut farther along, and a piece of gauze pulled through with long scissors. What that was all about I don't know. All of them had puffy faces or swollen feet. Those who went in there never came back out, that I did know. My uncle was lying inside there; his wife, too. They never returned to the camp. Nor did another uncle. All of them were finished off in there.

I cannot say for certain whether Mengele ever gave anyone a lethal injection. I wasn't there to witness it. There were rumours of it, but I don't know whether there was anything to them. He was a handsome, urbane man, and very affable – he was always laughing, never cross. If you look at photos of him, he always has a smile on his face.

Later, they started calling him the Angel of Death, as whenever you saw him you knew that death wasn't far behind. He would take a look around, call out some people's numbers and they would go with him, supposedly because of infectious diseases or for some other reason. He had a particular interest in twins. Thank God I wasn't one of those people.

As I said, he came to our sauna to shower and freshen up. I dusted down his boots and set them out ready for him. He put them on and went off to have a word with the kapo. We didn't talk in person; I was under strict instructions, like a soldier.

'Z 6084! Everything in order?'

'Yes, sir!'

That was all he ever said before leaving. Once he left some cigarettes behind on purpose. He wasn't supposed to give anything to anyone, of course. But he must have slipped something to the kapo and received something in return. The two of them were thick as thieves. It was like that with the other overseers, too. I wasn't allowed to be around while they were talking – all those conversations took place in the office, behind closed doors.[28] In other words, I couldn't eavesdrop, but to be honest I wasn't that interested anyway. It wouldn't have made any difference.

Mengele was someone whom practically everyone had to go to at some point. At the time, I never would have believed that he had such evil intent. It was only later, after 1945, that I began to hear more about his crimes.

I knew about his experiments, that he removed organs from the inmates at the camp – everyone did. They would say, 'Oh, look, here he is again. He's back to get what he needs from us.' People just said that he took things from corpses to experiment on them. That's how we described it. We didn't call it organ removal at the time.

I firmly believe that if doctors back then had been as advanced at organ transplants as they are today, none of us would have been worked to death. Quite the opposite, in fact. They would have said, 'We don't want you around, but we're not going to get rid of you; we're just going to lock you up.' We would all have lived a life of comfort, with the finest food and drink, sporting activities galore, events to go to, and so on. In other words, they would have sustained our bodies and nurtured our inner lives, too – our mind and spirit – on the understanding that they could make use of us whenever they wanted. If they needed organs, they could just say, okay, it's that one's turn tomorrow. Then they would have had endless fresh and flawless supplies straight from an abundance of people nourished and well cared for, under constant medical supervision, with every blood group present and correct. They'd even know whose heart would be the best match for a particular recipient. It would have been the finest repository of fresh meat imaginable.

Yes, that would have been better – at least millions of people wouldn't have been gassed and burned to ashes.

I'm not sure if I would still feel completely emotionless if I were to walk past a pile of corpses today, but in Birkenau I certainly got used to it. The bodies were simply part of our day-to-day: they were there, so we had no choice but to see them. And you couldn't miss them. I didn't even feel pity; I didn't think, 'Oh, those poor people.' There were were men, women and children, all just lying there. I remember one man – I think he was a Czech Roma – who, with another man, would grab the bodies by their arms and legs and toss them into an open truck like pieces of firewood. With children's bodies, they just took them by an arm or leg and hurled them away, as though carelessly discarding a piece of rubbish. The bodies whirled round as they flew through the air, before landing in the truck with a thump.

The pile of corpses lay right next to the sauna, behind the infirmary. The dead were dragged out there and piled up, deposited, stacked high, chucked away. Higher and higher. All of them naked. By the time evening fell, the pile was always around two metres high. And every evening a truck with a trailer came to pick up the pile and drive it over to the crematorium.

In such a place, you stop feeling altogether. People were past feeling, so to speak; they were numbed. If someone had come along and put them against the wall, they wouldn't have yelled, 'No! Somebody save me!' They wouldn't have cried or screamed. They wouldn't have made a sound. Such was our plight that we would have endured anything, like lambs being led to the slaughter. That was how utterly changed we were.

In a situation like that, people lose all sense of compassion. Your only instinct is to kick, beat and steal in pursuit of some advantage that might help you survive. If, when it was all over, you really looked at those people, really scrutinized their faces like I did, you would see that they were hardly people anymore; they were more like dumb beasts. Their faces bore an expression that I simply can't describe.

The camp stripped us of any sense of right and wrong. Our minds were destroyed and our nerves so tattered that we stopped seeing anyone else at all. If an inmate saw an opportunity to strike someone dead, they would seize it; there was no longer any inner voice stopping them. You saw the same thing with the kapos and the SS. It didn't matter whether it was a man, a woman or a child; they simply smashed them over the head so that the blood spattered everywhere. Sometimes they even hit them after they were dead. We're not talking about humans anymore.

The SS abused our women. Not in the block itself, but usually behind it or elsewhere. Afterwards, they shot them. One of my own relatives was shot in the head, but the bullet passed right through. She's still alive, but she's barely there at times, and she can't bear to be reminded of what she went through back then.

Behind the sauna was a ditch filled with water, then the fence, and beyond that the cordon of guards, strung out along the tracks. One warm day, the children went into the ditch to fetch water to clean the block. One of the guards shot at them. One child was hit in the arm, and a little boy in the stomach. I saw it with my own eyes, that boy clutching his intestines. They ordered a block curfew immediately after that.

There were people who broke out, including electricians who knew when the electric fence was switched off. The fence around the camp had a powerful current running through it. I remember one Sinti man who got caught. His parents and siblings, who lived in the same block, were beaten black and blue first. Then he was brought back in. They put him in immaculate new prison garb and laid him over the trestle. This was made of slats, with a rounded trough – it looked like the kind of thing that farmers once used to sort potatoes. In this case, there was a box underneath, into which the inmate's feet were wedged so he couldn't pull them out. He had to lie face down in the hollow, with his hands held out on either side. Then two men beat him from behind with thick leather whips. The SS did this at first. Eventually, they tired of the task and made the kapos or block elders carry on. You could see the blood running down the trousers of the man being beaten.

That man was tortured to death. They laid his body on a door and displayed him in the roll call yard, before carrying him around from block to block so that we could all see what would happen to anyone who tried to break out. He was a cautionary tale. Indeed, I don't think anyone made a bolt for it after that, if only for the sake of their family. There was no use, anyway. Wherever you might get to, they would catch you. We wouldn't have known where to run.

As I said, we were completely numb. There was one time, though, when we did fight back. That was when we learned that all of the Sinti were to be burned, every single one.

They had already rounded up the Russian Sinti in Block 23 and burned their bodies.[29] The story was that they had smallpox and would have infected us. The evening it happened, a few trucks pulled up and the SS jumped out with dogs, rifles and machine guns. They set about herding the people onto the trucks. We heard screaming, barking and crashes, and peered out through the openings in the roof; there weren't really any proper windows in the barracks.

The vehicles drove off. Before long we saw flames shooting up from the crematorium chimneys and the air was full of the smell of burning human flesh.

Whether those people were gassed or shot, I don't know. In Auschwitz, you stopped noticing the sound of machine-gun fire or gunshots.

I had a girlfriend in that block, named Sofie. She was the daughter of Didi, the block elder, and I had visited her just that day.

When the block elders learned that the rest of us Sinti and Roma were to suffer the same fate, they told us, 'Right, we need to be on our guard. The Camp Commander will be coming here to round us up.'

I have to give credit to Hans Koch and the other block elder, Wally, a stocky little man with blond hair, but savage all the same. He was in a relationship with a Sinti woman in the camp.

The plan was that I would be stationed on one side of the camp street, at the sauna, while my cousin Oskar – the one I went to school with – would be standing on the other. The block elders told us, 'When we signal you with our torches, run and knock on the door of every block. They already know what's going on.' If the SS had seen us, we would have been shot, but fortunately we went unnoticed. When we saw the signal we darted between the barracks, knocking on the doors, so that the block elders knew the SS were on their way. That done, we slipped back into our barracks. It wasn't long before Camp Commander Schwarzhuber and his men marched into the camp, with their machine guns and dogs on chains. He and his men walked a few blocks. We heard, 'Block elder reporting on behalf of Block 7, with 350 inmates! Nothing to report!' Schwarzhuber stopped at our block too, supposedly for a spot check on our record cards. No one came out.

We had prepared for this moment. All of us were armed with shovels, spades, hammers, pickaxes, hoes, forks and a whole arsenal of other tools that we had found about the place. Everyone thought, fine, if they want to take us out of here, then we'll sell our lives as dearly as possible. We won't just sit there for the taking. Maybe we could even get our hands on a machine gun, and then we'd stand more of a chance. The resistance was mainly made up of the block elders, the room orderlies and anyone who had any fight left in them. Lots of the block elders and kapos were in relationships with our women – some of them even had children born in the camp. They didn't want us annihilated; they were prepared to fight with us instead. This was a dangerous situation for the SS.

Schwarzhuber noticed that the lights had gone on in all the barracks, even over in the Polish and Jewish camps. The whole of Birkenau was lit up. Everyone was on the alert.

In the end, Schwarzhuber walked around a few blocks, then he and his men marched off without further ado. He evidently realized that if they went ahead, chaos would break out and people would resist. They might well have shot fifty or even a hundred of us, but what then? He knew we would have come after him, and he wouldn't have got away in one piece.

Those of us who had been living in Birkenau for a couple of years or more knew exactly what was going on. We weren't like the Jews who had just stepped off the train from different countries and set down their suitcases.

The mass extermination was called off, and we went on living in Auschwitz until August 1944, when a transfer was arranged.[30] All those still fit to work were to be put on a transport: 'Flex your muscles. If you've got what it takes, you're fit to work.' I was one of those selected.

I didn't want to go at first. 'I'm not leaving you, Mami,' I said.

She had a crowd of little grandchildren clinging to her; their parents were already gone.

'Come on, come with me,' I repeated.

'No, darling, you know I can't leave the little ones here alone. I just can't. They would be so scared . . . No, my sweet, I'll stay here, but you go.'

Then she herself called out, 'Orderly, there's another one here. My boy wants to go, too!' I did *not* want to go, but she kept urging me, 'Go on, get out of here!'

So I went, together with my cousin Oskar and his younger brother, Bodo. It later transpired that their father – my mother's brother Florian – and my Uncle Julius were on the transport, too. First, we were taken to the main camp at Auschwitz, where we waited. Then came the transport to Buchenwald.[31]

Chapter Seven

When we arrived at Buchenwald we were taken to a camp doctor. He sat at a table. We had to line up before him and take everything off. He looked us up and down and then gestured us to one side or the other.

Oskar and I were sent to one side and Bodo to the other. It was announced that those on Bodo's side would be going back to Auschwitz. Bodo was just a year younger than us, but they probably deemed him too scrawny. He began to cry; he had always been with his brother.

Oskar went over to Bodo's side and swapped his own number with that of another boy who wanted to stay in Buchenwald. Our numbers from Auschwitz were no longer valid in Buchenwald, you see; we had been given new ones. Mine was 74669. And these new numbers hadn't been tattooed onto us – they were just on our clothes. We had to sew them onto our trousers and below the left shoulder on our jackets.

So Oskar swapped places with the other boy, and he and Bodo went back to Auschwitz, to their deaths. I think he knew what would happen. The younger inmates who were sent back to Auschwitz were all exterminated there.[32]

If my brother had been sent back and I had had the chance to go with him, would I have done the same as Oskar? I don't know. But then, I was always alone. My mother was in the concentration camp at Ravensbrück; my father and brother Waldemar were in the camp in Bialystok, and my brother Max in Neuengamme. Only my grandmother had been with me, and then for only some of the time. Actually, I think it was just as well that I was on my own – it meant I didn't need to look out for anyone else. I decided what I wanted on my own terms and could follow those choices through. I'm sure that was one of the reasons I survived.

And with that, my childhood friends left. It wasn't your usual farewell – 'So long! Take care!' – there was none of that. It was, 'Step to! Quick march, quick march!'

'Bye, then,' I said. Then they were gone.

I suppose we might have imagined what would happen to those people, but the fact was we didn't even stop to think about it. Once you'd been in Auschwitz for two years, as I had, you sank into a state of apathy. We just let everything happen to us without putting up a fight. Take the injections they gave us, right up near the heart. No one drew back or protested, 'No, we're not having that!' We didn't know what it was, but it didn't occur to us to worry about it – we were too numb. Nothing mattered. Maybe it was just a vaccination; in fact, in must have been, or I wouldn't be sitting here now.

Some block elders arrived a little after us, and we learned that the entire Birkenau Gypsy Camp had been liquidated. All those who had remained in Auschwitz, including my grandmother and all my cousins – her grandchildren – had been wiped out. They killed every last one of them.

★

Oskar (right) und Bodo, cousins of Otto's

Kalutschabo and Barono, who were murdered in
Auschwitz-Birkenau on the night of 2 August 1944,
along with Otto's grandmother

I don't know exactly how long we were in Buchenwald. Was it a week? Three weeks? A fortnight, perhaps? I haven't a clue.

There was a bear pit there, with a real live bear inside. The man who looked after him was named Itzig.

The kapos and block elders at Buchenwald had various relations and acquaintances at Auschwitz, and they were keen to settle scores with any former Auschwitz kapos or block elders who had mistreated their kin. They knew exactly what had gone on in Auschwitz. They rounded up the overseers from Auschwitz, interrogated them and administered their punishment. One man was almost beaten to death. I don't know whether he had done what they accused him of – striking a pregnant woman dead, I think it was, or kicking her in the stomach. He fell to the ground, and one man went to finish him off with a rock to the head. At the very last second, he managed to dodge it and sprang to his feet. They continued to beat him, but he ran for his life and disappeared between the ranks of prisoners. He got lucky.

I was put to work; those in charge of the camp felt they had to keep the people busy somehow. We had to descend into a deep quarry. Once we got there, everyone heaved a rock onto their shoulders, then we had to trudge the long, hard path up to the top. There we would throw down our rocks and go straight back down into the quarry. We worked in a cycle, a never-ending chain. It was tough work: the rocks were angular and often enormous.

All of a sudden it was time to move on. Once again, a transport was put together and I was picked to go on it. This time it was heading to Dora, in the Harz Mountains. They had hewn tunnels out of the hills there and were manufacturing the V2 – the superweapon.[33]

I worked outside the tunnel to begin with. My crew had to cut a track into the rock. First, we opened it up by drilling, then laid fuses. The rock was detonated, and we cleared out the rubble.

The kapo was a great hulk of a man from Berlin. Hundekopp, his name was. He had a strikingly crooked nose, the kind you might see on a boxer or a pub landlord.

In Dora, I came across one of my cousins. He had actually been at Auschwitz, too, but I hadn't seen him while I was there. Before long, the two of us and my two uncles were sent on to the Ellrich subcamp.[34]

Chapter Eight

Roll call. 'Stand to attention!' We stood in line to be counted. That done, they assigned us to stone barracks. Every three or four men were given a blanket to share and paper sacks stuffed with wood shavings, ridden with fleas and manure. We slept. Upon waking the next morning, we were given half a loaf of bread, but not proper loaves; these were little hunks of dark army bread. Jam, too. At lunch, there was boiled potatoes and herrings but no water to drink. In the evening, we got another half a loaf and a slice of sausage or cheese. Just like in Auschwitz, those bread rations weren't quite what they seemed: the loaves were halved lengthways and crosswise, and then those brutes would cut a thick slice out of the middle. So what was supposed to be a quarter loaf was actually an eighth, and of course it wasn't enough.

We had to line up in blocks, then they'd divide us into *Kommandos* – work crews. Some would work in the tunnel, others out in the open air. I ended up in the Gawabau Kommando, which was tasked with levelling the ground for gas and water installations. We worked outside the tunnel, shovelling the rubble into the wagons. Then we would lay irrigation and drainage pipes. It meant trekking uphill and down, over and over again. I worked on the rockface with a jackhammer, too. I think we had to drill down 80 centimetres or so into the earth and rock. Needless to say, it was really hard work. Luckily, I wasn't a smoker, or I'd have been in trouble.

Roll call could happen at three or four in the morning – whenever they felt like it. Every morning, we would march out of the camp to the strains of a Sinti band. 'On the double!' They gave us orders, like soldiers. 'Company halt! Now forward! Quick march!' On other occasions, we would have to march on the spot and mark time.

We would march a little way to the railway station, a low building. When we got there, we climbed into cattle trucks, always in separate groups. I was in with the Russians. 'Get aboard!' We had to do it quickly: God help anyone who didn't make it inside fast enough. Any stragglers would get a beating.

The train carried us to the station at Woffleben.[35] 'Out you get!' Things were a bit calmer at this end. The train pulled away. We crossed the tracks and marched over to a big circular yard for roll call. Once everyone was assembled, we could march out to the work site in groups. I was working under Kapo Keutmann, who took a shine to me. The Russians or Poles nicknamed him Katschka – Polish for duck – because he was always waddling around on his crooked legs.

At midday, we usually headed back to the yard. Not always, though; sometimes we would eat lunch at the work site. A ladleful of stinging nettles with cabbage, potatoes, turnips, carrots – watery slop. There were bowls, but they were always being collected for washing up. *Miski*, the Russians called them. Getting hold of a *miski* was a complete ordeal. Then you had to stand there and hold it out, and then the man doling out lunch would dunk a full ladle into it, but when he whipped it out half the contents would slosh over the sides. You got whatever was left. If you said anything, he would bash you over the head with his ladle, so no one protested.

After eating, we marched back to work. There was a piece of iron hanging from a branch in the yard – a length of railway track, I think it was. 'Ding ding!' Anyone who didn't get straight back to work was searched out and given a thrashing. Needless to say, everyone rushed back right away. It's not like we could have ventured far in any case.

When our work was done, we would gather in the yard again and line up in rows of two or three. ''Ten-shun! Eyes front! Forward march!' The SS conducted spot checks, accompanied by blows and kicks. 'You, you and you – step out!' They'd search those men. If they found anything, the offending inmate would get a beating.

When the weather got colder, we found some empty cement bags, cut holes in the sides and at the top and started wearing them under our shirts. The only problem was that the guards had a habit of whacking us on the back with their sticks as we marched along. If you were wearing a cement back, they would hear it when the stick came down. 'You, step out! Take off your shirt!' More beatings would ensue if you were wearing a bag. They'd write down your number, too, so there was no escaping it. Supposedly, it was because of what the cement dust could do to you, but I don't know if there was any truth in that. I used to shake my bag out thoroughly to make sure it was clean, then turn it inside out. The wind couldn't get through, so it kept me warm.

They guards would check our feet, too. We didn't have socks, but occasionally someone would tear a blanket, and then everyone would rip it up, so we had strips of cloth to wrap around our feet. I never got caught, thank God.

I had a leather aviator-style hat with ear flaps, which I'd got in a trade at some point. That was lucky for me.

When we got back to Ellrich, there was another roll call, and then we could go to the washroom. Then tea, followed by bread, and that was it for the day. If it was warm, we could go for a little walk around the camp yard. When evening fell, the bell rang to signal that everyone had to be in their bunks.

It began all over again the next morning, with the ringing of the bell. 'Everybody out!' We were supposed to be outside the instant we heard those words. We got our bread and ate it or stuffed it under our shirts. Then it was straight to the washroom. There wasn't a moment to spare. We were ordered to wash, but the speed at which we had to do it made it almost impossible. We did it – the water was running, after all – but it was hardly thorough. Drinking from the taps was forbidden at Ellrich, too, due to the risk of typhoid, but everyone drank the water all the same.

There were about 35 of us in the Kommando, including my Uncle Florian, Oskar's father, and a couple of Russians, Sergey and Misha. Sergey was a foreman just like my uncle. Officially, all those Russians should have been in a POW camp, but they had been put in with us. I ended up learning a lot of Russian because they were around. There were Jews working with us, too, including Herr Meier, a short man.[36]

It was so bitterly cold that we would work hard to

get down into the earth, where it was warmer. 'Come on, Meier,' I said one time. 'Keep at it, so you can get down into the ground!'

'Do you think I'm crazy? Do you? I'm not going to work!' he said. 'There's no need to slave away, we just need to keep an eye out.'

'Fair enough,' I said, 'but do that and you'll freeze – look, you're already cold, aren't you?'

But he never listened to me; he preferred to stand there and shiver. He wasn't interested in helping other people out, either. So I dug for my own sake, so I could get down into the ditch. Being in there for a bit warmed you up, for one thing, and it was also your best chance of getting a break, no matter what the weather. When you were up on top, all you could hear was, 'Keep it up! No slacking!'

Nobody was allowed to stand still; being spotted not working earned you an instant beating. If I finished early, I had to help Meier so that he could finish, too, and then we could both move on together. We quarrelled about this a few times.

'Look, Meier, now I'm doing your work. You think that's fair?'

'Why are you going to all that effort?' he replied. 'Why bother?'

I noticed there was a particular spot where the soldiers would shovel hot ash out of their stoves. I found a cardboard box, tore one side off it and waited for my moment. I sprinted over – I couldn't get caught – and tipped the ashes into the box, then dashed back to my ditch. It worked best if I had managed to dig it deep enough not to be seen from the surface. I warmed my hands and feet in the hot ash.

Thinking back on it, there were all sorts of people in the Kommando, from lawyers to manual workers. Those common labourers were more robust; they could withstand the work. You could tell the intellectual types immediately: they had no idea how to hold or wield a shovel. Of course, I hadn't exactly come from a life of comfort and plenty, but one of poverty and hunger, so the grind of this existence didn't faze me like it did a professor now wandering around in prison garb.

If anyone addressed these once fine and upstanding members of society, they would respond in a calm, measured tone. That doesn't come over

so well in a prison camp, though. If you weren't in a
position of authority, you had to run with the pack,
pull together. But they just couldn't do it. They had
a delicate, sensitive disposition, and the experience
usually broke them. Not working earned them
beatings. Besides being in physical pain, they must
have been thinking, hang on, I'm a teacher, and here
I am being battered by a mere soldier or yard hand.
The soldiers hit hard, to be sure, but I have to say
that the prisoners hit harder. If someone wanted to
put their point across, they could be more brutal
than the guards.

I had a shovel that I used to seek out specially, as
it sat so nicely in my hand. Unusually, it had a small
blade, rather than a big one, which made striking
the earth and shovelling soil that much easier. I had
to shovel twice as much, but that wasn't any trouble.
At the end of work, I stashed it away somewhere so
that I'd be able to retrieve it again. When it was time
to fetch the tools, you see, everyone would run and
grab what was there. Some people didn't care what
they got, but I certainly did. Digging with this shovel
was almost a pleasure: it cut into the white, gravelly

earth perfectly. The kapo and general overseer set great store by smooth dug surfaces. You didn't need to support the ditch walls down to 80 centimetres, but if you went any deeper and your walls weren't flat, the trenches would cave in when you drove in the crossbeams. So the kapo wanted them pretty exact. To be honest, I felt pretty satisfied myself when the walls were nice and straight. Nice work, I thought.

I didn't have any shoes for a while. Instead, I took some cardboard, threaded some blasting wire through it and wrapped it around my feet.[37] Meier, on the other hand, had a spare pair of clogs, but he wanted bread, butter and sausage in exchange for them. 'Fine,' I said. 'But you'll have to wait – it'll take me a while to get those things.'

Then I noticed that he was taking those shoes out with him to work. 'Oh man,' I thought, 'if he gets spotted by the block elder, kapo or foreman, they'll get confiscated and he'll get a beating!'

One day, when I was sneaking my shovel out of its hiding place, I saw a trail in the snow leading away from the tool shack. I followed it and discovered

Meier's shoes. I popped them under my jacket and gave them to my Uncle Julius, who gave me his in return. They weren't much good anymore, but I sorted them out with wire and cardboard. I was always trying to make the best of everything.

Meier was onto me straight away. 'You've nicked my shoes!'

'What are you on about? I've no idea where your shoes are!'

'I saw the trail you left – those were your footprints!'

'It wasn't me. Someone else must have done it.' He never got them back.

I don't know what became of Meier. I'm not sure he'd have been happy to see me again.

One time, we needed to clear a hydrant that had become blocked up in the big freeze of winter 1944–45. 'Any volunteers?'

Otto reporting for duty. I climbed down the iron rungs into the deep, square shaft and started breaking off the ice to free the hydrant. Every now and then, I clambered back up to the top, stamped around a bit to get warm, then went back down again. I think the foreman and I untwisted it together in the end; he was a big guy and had the standpipe key. That got the water flowing again. I got a coupon worth one mark for my trouble, or maybe it was one mark fifty – the highest amount there was. That bought you some sauerkraut or tobacco.

Laying a pipe was usually a job for eight to ten men, but once we had a strapping man from East or West Prussia in the crew. 'I'll do it. Out of the way.' He lifted and laid it all on his own – a pipe that size! None of the rest of us could have managed anything like that.

In all my time in the camp, it seemed to me that the Russians had the greatest solidarity with one another. You didn't see that with the Sinti, the Roma, the Jews or anyone else; not even among the French.

That incredible team spirit was something I always noticed about the Russians. When we were ordered out of the camp and into the wagons, no sooner were they inside than they were hugging each other and singing rousing freedom anthems. The Wehrmacht or SS would come and knock the living daylights out of them with their rifle butts. But the Russians didn't let up. If one of them fell down, they'd get him back on his feet and keep on singing until the guards gave up, saying, 'Let's just leave them to it'.

The Russians were big guys – sturdy and heavyset – while the other prisoners were completely emaciated. This puzzled me, until I noticed that they were always popping these little triangular kernels in their mouths, like squirrels. I went over to them. 'What are those? Give me one.' They turned out to be beechnuts. And you know what, I too ended up eating them the whole time I was working outside. Both of my pockets were full of the things. They contain pure oil, so they give you strength.

Most importantly, I always made sure to keep myself clean. In the camp, we slept on paper sacks stuffed with wood shavings,full of lice, fleas and other bugs.[38] When I was working, I would take off my clothes. We were always making fires outside, to burn various things. I would hold my clothes over the fire, turning them in the heat, so that all the bugs and mites would fall out. I returned to the camp almost completely clean.

Outside, there was a little rivulet where I would wash myself at lunchtime if I had a moment spare. You had to be quick in the washroom – if you didn't manage to wash yourself quickly enough, you'd be pushed aside by others. The crowd were being beaten from behind, so they'd surge forwards. But I was quick and agile, and I wasn't very tall. If the SS started raining down blows on the prisoners, they'd catch the others first, not me. And I was good at making myself even smaller, which helped.

Ellrich was the only time I got to know an SS man, although 'got to know' is perhaps a bit strong. This bloke said something to me, and I replied. 'How come you speak German?' he asked. I suppose he wasn't used to hearing fluent German from the prisoners.

'I'm actually from Berlin,' I said.

He came a bit closer. 'Oh,' he said. 'Whereabouts in Berlin?'

I described where I had lived, but I don't think he could pinpoint it. Oh well, I thought. Anyway, we went on working, and he kept pacing back and forth. Then I found a wrapped-up piece of bread in my ditch. I wasn't sure whether it had come from him until a little later, when he threw me a big cigar butt. I took a drag on it and went all woozy. I thought I was going to keel over. Trying it was quite enough for me, I wasn't a smoker.

Soon after that, the guards needed one of us to go with them. The SS on the mountain had dogs, and the man who usually looked after them was ill. I imagine my SS man had spoken to the kapo and asked whether he could reassign me, just at lunchtimes, to feed the dogs. The kapo called me out of my ditch and took me over to the SS man. I said my number and, 'Reporting for duty!'

'The dogs need fresh water and their lunch. Here's some dog biscuits. They get one with each meal, or sometimes two.'

'Yes, sir! You can count on me.'

I had to do things by the book the first day, as the SS guard was watching me the whole time. But I obviously did the job to his satisfaction, as after that he stopped paying so much attention.

Whenever I gave the dogs their lunch – thick slices

of sausage and bits of meat – I thought, 'What we wouldn't give for a meal like that!'

One time, the SS guard wasn't anywhere to be seen and the dogs were unsettled and refusing to eat. I took my mess cup, put their food in it and hid it under my shirt. Later, when I was safely back in my ditch – it wasn't far – I ate my fill and then dished out the rest to the others. Dog biscuits taste like nuts. They never tasted better, let me tell you.

I don't know how long I was assigned to that job, but I ate my way back to a decent weight while I had it. It gave me a new determination to survive.

The Gawabau Kommando had a non-military supervisor who took two or three of us to his house a couple of times to lay some drainage pipes. An SS guard came along, too. While I was there, his wife – or maybe she was the housekeeper – gave me a glass of milk. I wasn't allowed to take anything from the people living there, and they weren't supposed to speak to us, either. I was toiling away outside the window, and she put the milk down on the sill. At first, I just carried on working, but then I drank it. It was as though the sun had suddenly burst out from behind a cloud. The sheer joy of it – knowing that there were still good people in the world.

During my time working on the Woffleben tunnels, I saw three men hanged.

We were often made to march from Ellrich to the train station, where we would board goods wagons and travel to Woffleben. After alighting, it was another short walk to the square. To the right lay the tunnels where they were working on the V2. Everything was out of bounds and guarded by dogs and sentries with machine guns. There were a lot of lookout towers there, too.

It was all because of a little drive belt. The conveyor systems in the tunnels were powered by a motor, which had a short drive belt, about 40 centimetres square. The drive belt in question was completely worn down, so it could no longer be used; in fact, it had already been replaced. So the prisoners cut it up and nailed it to the bottom of their wooden clogs to make them last longer.

The Nazis made short work of them. In the yard, they set up a pole on two stands, like the rails you hang rugs over to beat dust out of them. The pole had rings screwed into it, as I recall. A group of soldiers marched in. They weren't SS, but Luftwaffe ground crew, with a seagull on their uniform. Most of them had yellow collar tabs, some red, again with seagulls on them. Later, they would start wearing grey senior and junior squad leader uniforms of the SS. One of them read aloud from a sheet of paper. 'Due to sabotage . . .' (I remembered that I had once been charged with sabotage, too) '. . . perpetrated on the property of the people . . .' It continued in that vein, with a whole litany of offences.

We all had to leave our work and line up around the gallows. The SS, with their dogs and machine guns and guards, looked down on everything from above. The three men were sentenced to death under martial law, effective immediately. I think they were a Pole, a Russian and a Sinti, but I can't remember exactly.

They each had to stand on a box. A piece of wood was wedged in their mouths and secured at the back of their heads with a piece of red blasting wire. This was used to tie their hands behind their backs, too. Once the soldier had read out the verdict, the boxes were pulled away, leaving them hanging there. The hangman was a kapo at the camp, who had been told that if he hanged the three men, he would be free to go home. He did as he was asked.

The men thrashed about a little bit, and then it was all over. We had to line up column by column, with the kapo in front, and march past the dead men, looking up at them. Anyone who didn't look closely enough was taken out of the line and shoved against the corpses.

They were taken down a little later. Afterwards, I happened to be working in the area and I saw the bits of wood and wire lying there. I picked them up and put them in my pocket. I'm not sure whether I had all three of them, but I remember thinking, 'Okay, now you have proof.'[39] I carried those wooden gags around in my pocket for weeks.

As I said, we would take the train home at the end of the day and travel back to work in it in the morning. There was an elderly man and his son in our Kommando. I'd been ill and hadn't eaten my potatoes.

So when the old man saw me peeling them, he asked for one, but I wouldn't give him any. We all got the same amount, after all. He took my peelings, though. Then my uncle and I heard him say to his son, 'Ah, my boy, no matter what we do, we're not getting out of here alive. We should take our own lives. We could throw ourselves under the train.'

'No, no,' said the boy. He didn't want to.

By the time we were on the train to the work site the next day, I had forgotten all about it. But then Otto Schmelzer – who's dead now – and I heard that something had happened with the train.

Kapo Katschka came over to us. 'Come with me, you two. Get a stretcher.' In fact, we ended up carrying a big tub that they used for mixing mortar. There were four of us: Oskar and I, the kapo and an SS guard. That was when we heard that someone from our Kommando had jumped under the train.

When I look back, it strikes me just how often I witnessed such things.

We walked along the tracks and there he was – a piece here, a piece there, another one over there. We had to put them all in the tub. 'You know what?' I said to Otto. 'He probably did it because I wouldn't give him a potato.' That's how it felt, at least. I thought, 'If only I'd known, then of course I would have given him one. But it's too late now.'

His boy was all alone now. After the war, he went to live in Hamburg. I heard from him and went to visit him there, but we didn't talk about his father's death: it was still too raw.

I wouldn't be able to talk about it now if so many years hadn't passed since. At first, it affected me so badly that I had to stop every three words or so. And I couldn't talk about my parents or brothers and sisters at all; the words simply wouldn't come out.

On those festive occasions when people like to get together, I've shut myself away or wept into my drink. But drinking only makes things worse. It's only now that I can look back and talk about it properly. There's no getting over it, though. I've kept the photographs of my family all this time and still light candles around them. That's the only consolation I have left: thinking of my loved ones.

How the SS and, I suppose, Germans like you or me could have done what they did is beyond me. Nobody can understand it. No one knows how people can act like that. Even if you're ordered to do something, it doesn't mean you have to do it, at least not to the letter. Even if you're ordered to do something, you might still be able to let someone go. What I'm saying is, I'm sure there were plenty of German soldiers who were good people, but most were not; most were evil. Before, I had always looked up to the German soldiers I had seen on the bus or at the railway station.

Thinking back on Marzahn . . . there were soldiers stationed near us, manning the anti-aircraft guns. They would shoot at any attacking planes, and I found it pretty thrilling. I didn't see them as a threat. I used to have lunch with them, in fact. They had nothing against me, even though they knew that I was a Sinti from the camp. There was no animosity there. But I came to experience just how evil people can be, in the worst possible way.

In Ellrich, they would lock men in a standing cell if they'd committed some misdeed. When it was opened again, they would usually fall out dead, although some did survive it. The bodies always lay between Ellrich and the motor pool where my cousin worked. I used to go and see him quite often; he would help me out with bread or some soup every now and then. He's dead now, too.

Anyway, that's where the bodies were laid out. Now, at some point someone noticed that their genitals – their testicles – were always missing. No one could explain why, so the SS kept watch on the corpses. That's how they caught the Russian who had been cutting off the testicles and eating them.

We had to line up in the camp yard for roll call. The commander declared, 'This man has been nibbling on these corpses.' He said that this could lead to an outbreak of disease and contaminate the entire camp. The SS made the Russian prove that he had really done it. They put him on a platform, and there he took those parts of the corpse, added some salt and devoured them.

In a judicious tone, the Commander said, 'I would be all too willing to sentence him, but I'm not going to. Instead, I'm going to turn him over to his fellow inmates.'

Those fellow prisoners were Russians, too. No sooner had the Commander spoken those words than the Russians hauled the man down from the platform and laid into him, roaring with fury. They tossed him up in the air and then stepped apart so that he crashed down on the ground. Again and again they did it, until he was dead.

He ate those body parts that he had cut off, in front of the assembled prisoners, for all of us to see. He did it. I, Otto Rose, saw it with my own eyes, and live to tell the tale. But why the Russian did it – whether out of sheer hunger, complete desperation or madness – I will never know.

One day, some planes flew low over Woffleben. The word was that they were English or Canadian. 'Maybe they've come to free us,' we thought excitedly. We waved and threw our caps up in the air. Suddenly, the planes wheeled around and came back, this time in a nosedive. I threw myself between some carts, face-down in the mud as the dive-bombers came at us, shooting with their machine guns.

The rumour was that the Russians were getting closer. One morning, the camp commander came into the yard at roll call and announced, 'Anyone who volunteers for the SS will get their freedom, a uniform and enough to eat.' After some brief training, they would be expected to fight. As young and naive as I was, I was keen to sign up. Then I would at least be out of there, with a weapon in my hand and the chance to defend myself.

I was all ready to put myself forward, but my uncle – long dead now, God bless him – grabbed me by the collar and gave me a clip around the ear, saying, 'Have you gone mad, boy? You can't go and be one of them now that the Russians are almost here and things are almost over!' I fell back into the line.

Lots of men volunteered to join the Dirlewanger Brigade – that's what they called them.[40] One of them was Ernst Ewald, one of my mother's cousins. He was taken prisoner by the Russians. What a fate: to be sent to a camp, volunteer in the hope of freedom, and then end up in a Russian camp.

We could already hear Russian gunfire. This is it, we thought – freedom is nigh! We're getting out of here! But instead we were herded into cattle wagons.

We were driven back and forth for I don't know how long. They didn't know what to do with us; none of the other camps wanted us. It's a miracle they didn't decide just to blow us up. I think we must have spent several weeks in those wagons – me, my Uncle Florian, Uncle Julius and my cousin from the motor pool. The train kept stopping and starting.

There were no toilets in the wagons, of course – nothing but straw. Sometimes, fresh straw would be added to the wagons, but it was still unbearable. So many people died in there. The stench and filth were incredible. No one was allowed to leave the train; anyone who so much as leaned out of the wagon would be shot immediately by the guards. Lots of people were killed that way.

There was one occasion when we did come out, during an air raid. The guards – those big, menacing fellows – threw themselves into ditches, with their steel helmets on their heads. I clambered out and crawled under the wagon. Then I saw that other prisoners were running towards piles of swedes and beetroot in the fields. I did the same. The SS started shooting and people began falling all around me, but I didn't get hit. Maybe they were just firing randomly.

I managed to snatch up a swede or two. By that stage, I barely had the strength to lift a thing. I dashed back, crawled under the wagon and climbed back in. My uncles helped me up. They were so happy to see me. 'Here,' I said. 'I've got you something!' They started on the swedes right away. We shared them between us and ate. Then they swapped the rest of my haul for tobacco and had a smoke. I didn't smoke, so I had no need of tobacco, but there they were, smoking away. I can laugh about it now, but it wasn't remotely amusing at the time. My strength was almost gone, my arms just skin and bone.

Once, when we were standing next to the tracks, I spotted a piece of greaseproof paper with some smoked herring bones inside. Goodness only knows how long they'd been sitting out there in the sun. I would have gobbled them up in an instant, but my cousin grabbed them from me and threw them away.

We weren't human anymore; we were more like wild animals. The soldiers would give us one loaf of bread between fourteen men. What use was that? Each of us got one meagre slice, plus a spoonful of tinned meat each day.

When we were finally let out, we still had a way to walk. The valiant soldiers shot all those who couldn't muster the strength. What evil men they were.

Chapter Nine

When we arrived in Bergen-Belsen, we were assigned to big stone buildings that had once been army barracks.[41] Apart from that, it was more of the same, with room orderlies and so on.

I was pretty much done for by this point – nothing but skin and bone. We foraged for potato peelings behind the kitchen with sticks, then toasted them on the fire, even though they were already blue with mould. We had lost all our scruples around food. If we found a bone lying around, we didn't care where it had come from – a dog or something else – we just broke it open and sucked out the marrow. Anything for a bit of taste.

In a show of magnanimity, the SS suddenly

announced that we were each going to be given a big tin of meat. They didn't have any bread, they said, but they would arrange for some to be delivered. Maybe better times are on the horizon, we thought.

All of a sudden, the top brass scarpered and the Hungarians were put in charge, almost overnight. But when it came to guarding us, they weren't very vigilant at all. Everyone just went wherever they wanted. An SS guard was even lynched on the camp street by a few men who still had some strength left in them. I didn't witness it myself, but I heard his scream, as it happened right by my block. An SS guard had his pistol stolen and the prisoners ran riot. As the allied troops advanced, the last remaining guards did a runner.[42]

Any inmates who were able to make a dash for freedom did, too. My Uncle Julius said, 'We're not staying another second. Let's go.' But I couldn't walk. My clogs had been chafing, and my left ankle was painfully swollen and oozing with pus. The other problem was that my uncle and the men he was leaving with were planning to cross a river; I assume it was the Elbe. I had never learned to swim, so I couldn't go along with them – I would have been a liability. What's more, I was still terribly afraid of making a mistake somehow.

The buildings we were in had already emptied out. I lay there, delirious, with no idea what was going on around me. My mind was so ravaged that I didn't know up from down.

Walking down the road that ran through the camp was practically a death sentence, but I left our block, nonetheless. I staggered down the road and went into another block. There I climbed the stairs to the attic, where I found a rocking horse. Desperately weak and sick, I dragged it down all those steps and back down the road to our block, back to my room. I positioned it in front of my box bunk and lay down, with that rocking horse right there beside me. Nobody was shouting orders; no one was saying anything any more.

And then the Allied troops came into the camp, and we were liberated. I didn't know what nationality they were – British, American or Russian. German soldiers were the only ones I had known. Yes, I knew them all right.

The Allies confiscated everything. We weren't allowed even a morsel from our tins of meat; apparently they were all poisoned. We were furious that they had taken our tins away – we couldn't understand what was going on. Instead, they gave us dry bread or crispbread, and cooked up chocolate pudding or something for us.

I was just as scared of the Americans and the British and the Russians as I had been of German soldiers and the SS. I didn't know the first thing about these people, after all. Did they wish us harm or had they come to help? I had no idea. I was still too young to get my head around it all.

Eventually, I managed to get back on my feet. I set off with my Uncle Florian, my cousin Willi and another man whose name I can't recall. We were still in our prison uniforms and clogs, still nursing our long-held fear in the very marrow of our bones. We knew nothing of what was out there. There was shooting all around: the rattle of a machine gun here, someone firing there. Nothing was certain.

We headed towards the Lüneburg Heath. As we made our way across a little bridge over a river two armed men came towards us, dressed in short jackets and caps. Now I know that they must have been English, but I didn't back then. They came up to us and said, in English, 'Line up on the bridge!' They lined us up along the parapet of the bridge, side by side. This can't be good, we thought. Now we've had it. 'But why?' we asked. 'We haven't done anything wrong!'

We couldn't understand what they were saying, and they didn't understand us either. 'Oh God,' I thought, 'I've managed to survive this whole time, I've come through all that awfulness and misery, overcome all those obstacles, only to be shot by these guys!' But we lined up as instructed, as though we didn't much care. We didn't fight it. No one refused or bothered to ask the soldiers again why they were doing this.

One of them started taking off his submachine gun. The Brits all had these little contraptions that looked like tin toys. I closed my eyes and waited for the bang, for the end. But nothing happened. I peeked through my eyelids, then finally allowed myself to open my eyes fully. I saw the soldier hand his submachine gun to his companion, reach into his breast pocket, pull out a little camera and take a picture of us. I felt a massive weight fall away as I realized that they weren't out to hurt us. There are no words to describe the feeling of having your life given back to you.

The soldier took a few snaps of us and laughed. Then he reached into his pocket again and pulled out a slender carton containing four cigarettes. He gave one to each of us.

I'd give anything for that photo today.

We continued on our way, but we hadn't gone far before we spotted a field kitchen on a little hill, swarming with soldiers. They had all their guns set up, and it was clear that they weren't German.

'I'm going over there,' I said.

'No way, just keep going. They'll arrest you!'

But I made my way over regardless and showed the Brits or Americans – whoever they were – the number on my arm.

They gave me biscuits, soup and chocolate pudding. I ate it all up, then they handed me another packet, presumably from their rations. I tucked my jacket into my trousers and retied the waistband, holding the packet in place.

I went back down the hill. My uncle and the others were already a little way ahead, so I whistled. They saw me and stopped to wait. 'Here,' I said. 'Have some of this!'

You can imagine how hungrily they dug into the food, eating with both hands. For the first time in ages, we could eat our fill. It was a hearty meal that left us happy and content.

We walked another three kilometres or so, and then I fell down unconscious.

Chapter Ten

When I woke up, I was in Celle. I was lying in a room where beds had been set up, with Red Cross nurses in attendance. An alarm clock or some other kind of ringing sound woke me up. My instinct was to jump out of bed straight away, as I was primed to do. A ringing bell or similar to me meant, 'Quick, up! Get outside, fast as you can!' It was a signal for me to be on my spot, ready for work. I struggled to sit up, but soothing hands gently pushed me down.

'There's no need to be afraid anymore. You're free. It's over. It's over.' But that was hard for me to grasp.

I was given only a very little to eat, bit by bit; otherwise I probably would have died. They nursed me back to health slowly, like a child. My only desire was to eat and drink. And such kindness! The nurses were so sweet and caring. It wasn't just food and drink we needed, of course, but also sustenance for our souls to heal.

After a few weeks, I was feeling stronger again. The fear that had been breathing down my neck had subsided. I no longer expected to be murdered and my body burned. We started to look around and realized that the danger had been averted, at least for now. We were safe. I set off with my cousin Willi. Later, he vanished somewhere around Cologne, never to be seen again.

My uncle and the other man who had been travelling with us said, 'We're not going back to Berlin just yet. We'll stay here for now.'

'I have to see whether anyone from my family is still alive,' I said. 'I have to find out what happened to my brothers and sisters.' My cousin was keen to do the same.

Berlin couldn't be all that far, surely? We headed in that direction, marching across the Lüneburg Heath for days and sleeping wherever made sense at the time. There was unrest and looting everywhere.

We could hear shooting, too, but couldn't tell where it was coming from. We saw lots of people who had got weapons from somewhere, but we ourselves were unarmed.

I remember that one day we came to a farmhouse and asked for food – not in the polite way you normally would, but demanding it. The woman of the house sat in the living room with her children clustered around her. She was crying pitifully. Looters had ransacked the place, leaving her and her children with nothing. We felt sorry for her – they weren't to blame for the war, after all.

She said that if we wanted to eat with the children and were fine with the little she had, she would be willing to share it with us. It wasn't much of a meal – bread, potatoes and curd cheese – but it was a gourmet meal as far as we were concerned. We sat down and tucked into the feast, which left us nice and full.

We stayed there for a few days; perhaps it was even as long as two weeks. We slept in the house and the woman cooked for us. We ate with the children. It was absolutely wonderful.

We weren't just sitting around the house all day,

either: while we were there, we managed to catch a horse. My cousin and I were walking across a field when we saw a horse coming towards us.

'Hey, look at that! You go that side; I'll go this side.'

We approached it slowly and cautiously, the way you have to if you don't want a horse to take fright and bolt. Little by little, step by step, we crept up to it, one of us on either side. We were talking to it softly all the while, our hands outstretched. Then we had it. We knew what to do: reach across its nostrils with one hand, while grabbing its ear with the other. Then it can't get away. We didn't have any kind of rope or leash, nothing. Grabbing a horse by the nose is like putting a bridle bit on it. We calmed it down and led it back to the farm, where we gave it some food. Later, we hitched the horse to a three-wheeled plough, took turns sitting on it and ploughed a little section of field.

We talked to the woman and played with her children during our stay. I think my experiences on the farm helped shape my views from then on. When I first arrived there, I was full of hatred and intent on killing. I wanted to murder everyone, not just those who had tormented us in the camp. I thought, 'You lot never accepted that we were Germans, so when we get out, we'll kill you Germans in turn.' At that point, we were still too weak to be a danger to anyone, but the thought was there. Over time, though, those feelings changed.

I remember how I used to visit the Monastery of Christ the King as a young boy. I was an altar boy for a while, and the priests in charge were keen for little Otto to enter into the seminary. Father Petrus, Director Trüding, Brother Williges and the whole lot of them saw something in me. I was keen to give it a try myself, and I think it would have happened if I hadn't ended up in the camp.

Being with this woman and her children made me remember my faith. Had we killed them, there would have been no repercussions. We could have just continued on our way. By the time that I left them, I was a different person, even if I hadn't been altogether restored to normality. I was still a bit messed up in the head.

As I say all of this out loud, I can feel a fear rise up in me. The thought that I could have killed someone always hits me like a physical sensation. It's never left me.

We were reluctant to leave, but I knew we had to get to Berlin, so we set off again, trudging across the Lüneburg Heath. One hot day, we came to an inn, which was completely uninhabited. We found some proper malt beer in there, so we drank our fill, then packed the remaining bottles in an army knapsack; there were always heaps of these lying around by the side of the road. We stashed a loaf of bread and a big tin of jam in there, too, along with our spoons from the camp and some knives.

We followed a forest trail, which led to a small paved road. Then we came to a sudden stop. A convoy of trucks was driving past, including an American jeep driven by a man whose leg was sticking out at the side. At that moment, I happened to be drinking from a bottle of malt beer. I waved at him with the bottle.

He slammed on the brakes, jumped out of the truck and came running towards us. We span around and started running, too. The terror that we both felt at that moment!

'What did you do that for, you idiot? He must have

thought you were threatening him! Now he's coming back to beat us up!'

We did our best to get clear, but the man had such long legs that he was on us in no time. He snatched the bottle from my hand, pushed my head back and held the bottle to my mouth. I drank.

When he saw that I was drinking, he took the bottle from my lips and drained it.

'Do you have any more?' he asked. He was speaking English, but we understood him immediately. We would have given him anything. He took our bottles, drained them, too, then threw them away just like the first. Then he took us over to his truck and gave us each a parcel.

We opened them up to find biscuits, powdered milk and cigarettes inside. Neither I nor my cousin smoked at that point; I only took it up when I was back out in the world.

We crossed the road and continued tramping on and on through the forest. Suddenly, we saw a carriage in the distance, coming towards us with shouts of 'Gee up!' and an almighty clattering. It was rocking dangerously from side to side and the horses were drenched with sweat. Russians. But these weren't uniformed officers; they were former inmates like us, all completely drunk. They stopped, jumped down and came towards us with their guns at the ready.

'*Stoy*!' they shouted. 'Hands up!'

One of them was wearing boxing gloves, real ones.

'We were in the camp!' we shouted. We showed them our numbers.

'Take off your knapsacks!'

We opened up our knapsacks and they looked inside, spotting the jam. They cut open the can with proper daggers. They started eating it all up themselves at first, but soon they stuck a spoonful in each of our mouths, too. When they were done, they leapt back onto the horses and into the carriage, made a hasty U-turn – bump, crash – and galloped away again.

We continued on our way and eventually came to the camp at Salzwedel. It had once been a military airbase, but now it was a British reception camp. We were issued with passports there, with our fingerprints in red ink.

While we were there, we met lots of other former prisoners – men and women from Hungary, Romania, the Netherlands. They had made it there from all over the place. Once again, we stayed in barrack huts, but our rations were far more plentiful now. There was enough to eat and drink, even brown sugar from burlap bags. I stuffed my pockets full so I could gorge on it all the time.

We also met two Czech girls. One of them was named Pietka. We were keen to leave the camp, so we set out for Berlin, together with the two girls. But we had only gone a little way before we got into a disagreement about whether to go on.

'We'll land ourselves right back in hot water.'

So we turned back. At least in Salzwedel there was an incredible violinist, so we could make music.

We were registered as resident there, if only because of the food supplies, but although we had everything given to us in Salzwedel, we weren't exactly free either.

We could go wherever we wanted, but we only ever came across former prisoners, like us. And for as long

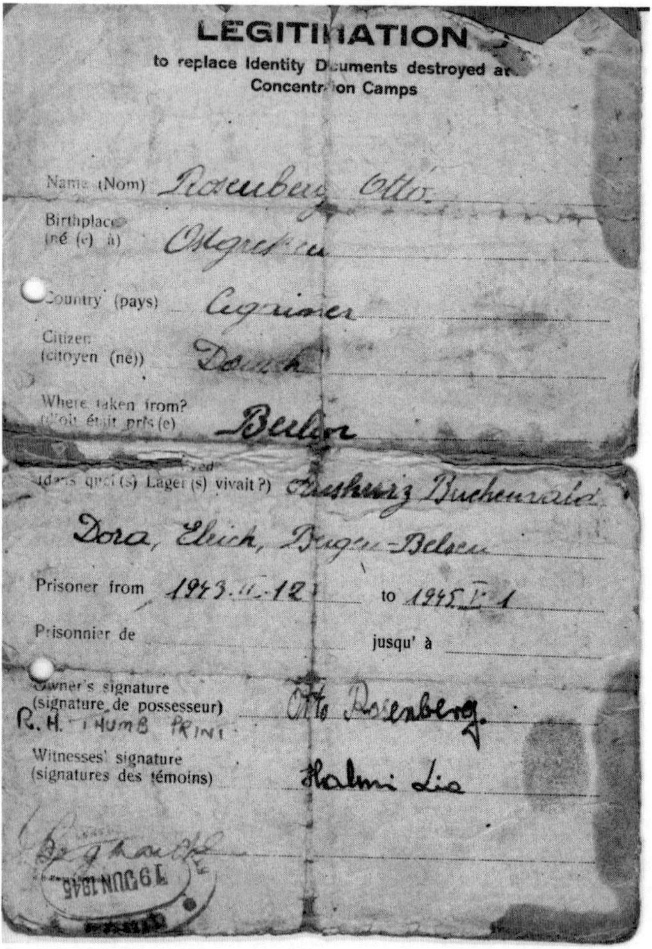
LEGITIMATION

to replace Identity Documents destroyed at Concentration Camps

Name (Nom) Rosenberg Otto

Birthplace (né (e) à) Ostpreussen

Country (pays) Zigeuner

Citizen (citoyen (ne)) Deutsch

Where taken from? (d'où était pris (e)) Berlin

(dans quel (s) Lager (s) vivait ?) Auschwitz Buchenwald Dora, Ellrich, Bergen-Belsen

Prisoner from 1943.III.12 to 1945.V.1

Prisonnier de jusqu' à

Owner's signature (signature de possesseur) Otto Rosenberg.

R.H. THUMB PRINT

Witnesses' signature (signatures des témoins) Halmi Lia

19 JUN 1945

Otto's provisional ID papers, Salzwedel

as we kept encountering those camp inmates, our imprisonment wasn't at an end. We had all suffered the same sort of torment, although some of the girls may have had even worse memories than I did, as they had been raped by the SS or other soldiers. To think that our soldiers, especially the highly decorated ones, whom you might assume were intelligent folk you could look up to, would turn out to be murderers and criminals who raped defenceless victims!

In the end, I started out for Berlin again with another girl, from Kispest in Hungary. When we got to the Elbe, the British were on one bank, I think, and the Russians on the other. They had set up a makeshift bridge and there were lots of cars standing around. We boarded a train, but the Russians hauled us out for interrogation. Luckily, I could speak a little Russian, and they let us on our way.

Chapter 11

When we arrived in Berlin, the first thing I did was to hike over to Marzahn with my knapsack. But the camp was empty and mostly burned down. The house where our teacher liked to go to visit the farmer's wife was still standing opposite the camp square, but she wasn't there anymore. Now Frau Schwarz, the wife of the man who used to have a shop at the camp, lived there. She, her husband Walter and his elderly mother had run the shop, but only her daughter was around when I visited. 'The camp got bombed,' she said.

There had been no air-raid bunkers in Marzahn, of course; I'd witnessed air raids there myself. In fact, I had visited the anti-aircraft gunners every day and often cadged some food from them. They were always happy to share their bread with me. I might have been something of a running joke for them, for all I know.

Although the camp had been firebombed, the Schwarz's daughter told me that she thought the people who lived there had fled from the attack into the fields. She thought that some of them were now camped out near the cattle stockyard in Friedrichsfelde. I went looking around the allotments in Friedrichsfelde.

'Are there any gypsies living around here?'

Yes, here and there, came the reply.

There were a few in Karlshorst who hadn't been sent to a concentration camp, and they gave me a few more pointers. That's how I was reunited with my Aunt Camba, with whom I'd grown up at my grandmother's. We were always very close as a result, and still are to this day. She was overjoyed to see me.

I moved into the shed where my aunt lived with my uncle, Paul Franzen, and their children.

'Come on in, boy.'

'And my girl?'

'Yes, yes, it's fine. Come on in.'

I had nightmares every night and would jump up crying and screaming. My aunt thought I'd gone mad – 'Calm down, for goodness' sake!' She had only been in Marzahn; she had never been sent to Auschwitz or Ravensbrück. I'm not sure why.

We lived there in Friedrichsfelde for quite a while, but I'm not sure whether I was ever officially registered there. Eventually, we moved to housing in Britz that had formerly been reserved for combat veterans.[43] The original residents were all Nazis, but many of them had done a runner or been thrown out, leaving some of the houses empty. We were assigned to one of them, up on Grüner Weg, so that's where I lived, with my aunt, her husband and my girl.

The owner of the house, a Frau Ebert, came by to visit us. We made it clear to her that we weren't interested in staying in her house for ever, so she would be able to move back in at some point. We could have insisted on our rights, but what would have been the point, really? That wasn't our intention. Most of the people who lived there had been in thrall to the

Nazis. They said hello and spoke to us easily enough, but they made us feel nervous.

I registered with the authorities and had to go to the employment office to get ration cards. They put me straight back to work, right after '45! And it was laying pipes, of all things – no different from what I'd been doing in the concentration camp. It was all too much for me to manage. 'I can't do this anymore,' I told them.

They sent me to the medical officer. 'You can't just refuse work,' he said. 'You'll have to register as disabled.' That was how fast they came down on us again and insisted that we slave away. They were the same old Nazis in the same old jobs. They wanted to see my birth certificate, even though all my papers had been taken from me. And they did it all so harshly! We were still pretty scared by them, to be honest. It felt as though they were still in charge, and we needed to hold our tongues.

My girl didn't understand a word of German; she only spoke her own language and Romany. She was Roma, not Sinti, and she had no desire to stay in Berlin.

★

Whenever we heard a rumour about another concentration camp survivor turning up, we would go off looking for them. Most of the time it came to nothing, but on one of those quests I met some Polish women who had been in Ravensbrück. I asked them if they knew a Katza, my mother.

'Katza?' they said. 'Oh yes, we know her.'

'Is she alive or dead, do you know?'

'She's alive. She said she was going to Berlin.'

Can you imagine what it was like to suddenly hear that my mother was still alive? I tracked her down.

'My son! My son's alive!'

'What happened to the others?' I asked.

'We haven't seen a trace of them. They're all dead.'

I lived with my mother for a while after that. My girlfriend was with us, but she was still hankering to go back to Hungary. '*Németországban azaz nem jó*,' she would say – it's no good staying here in Germany. It didn't help that she couldn't communicate with anyone but me.

'Your bloody Nazi mob!' were her only words of German. She had suffered terribly, poor thing. One day, she told me that she was determined to go

Luise Herzberg, Otto's mother, *c.*1950

back to Hungary. We knew a German man nearby who spoke fluent Hungarian so he talked to her and arranged everything with the consulate. She wouldn't be stopped.

My mother tried to talk sense into her, but to no avail. At that point, my mother herself was very ill. She had contracted tuberculosis in the camp and would later die as a result of the disease.

I told my girlfriend that I wouldn't be able to go to Hungary with her. 'If anything happens, I won't be there to protect you.' She packed my camera, jacket and belongings regardless, and as she was leaving, she murmured my name over and over again.

'Okay,' I said. 'I'll follow you later.'

I didn't hear from her again until after my mother died, and then we lost touch.

We would go out foraging from the house on Grüner Weg, often staying out all day and night, before returning home triumphantly with a great big sack of potatoes, which fed everyone, my aunt and mother included.

I did some black-market business on the side as well, often on Alexanderplatz. Like Rosenthaler Platz, it was a bustling hub where everything was traded or bartered, legally and illegally. White bread, rye bread, cigarettes, leather jackets, rings – you name it, they were all being bought and sold there. Of course, the German police would make regular raids, driving up, jumping out of their vehicles and snatching up people's wares.

There were loads of returned soldiers standing around in their grubby uniforms and squashed caps. I'd always give them a little something, even though I might just as well have said, 'Ugh, get lost, you disgusting brutes!' But I could never have done it; I felt so sorry for them, you see. You'd see men missing arms and legs. I'd exchange a few words with them every now and then.

'The fatherland did this,' one of them told me.

'So don't you get any money off them?' I asked. Evidently, none of that had been sorted out yet. I learned that the man's wife had run off with someone else and didn't want to see him again; she wouldn't even let him back in their apartment. Oh God,

I thought, the things that man has had to go through, first in the war and then at home.

'I was on the other side,' I said. 'In a concentration camp.' Some people did acknowledge that they'd heard about the camps, but they always claimed to have had nothing to do with them personally.

'I was at the front,' he replied.

If you go to a cemetery, then everywhere you'll see tombstones with inscriptions commemorating wonderful mothers, excellent fathers and God-fearing aunts. But where are all the bad people? Next time you're in a cemetery, cast your eye over the gravestones and those glowing words of praise. Apparently, they were all good people, the lot of them! Can that possibly be true?

Berlin was a heap of rubble. Just like everyone else, we were helping to rebuild it, dusting off stones and putting them in a pile. We didn't get much for our labour. The friend I was with wasn't putting in much effort and got pulled up on it: 'Oi, Mr Adler, you have to do your bit, just like everyone else!'

'Have you gone soft in the head?' he retorted. 'What's wrong with you? I've made it here from a concentration camp and now I've got to work on a construction site? You think I destroyed all this, do you? The ones who wrecked it all need to get over here and rebuild it.'

We went on cleaning stones and clearing debris; Berlin was our hometown, after all. But it wasn't easy at times.

There was no talk of compensation or reparations back then. When the time for that finally came, in the fifties, I had to go to the district court, only to be told that I wasn't a real German and had no ties to Berlin.

'He's a gypsy. Roving spirit and all that. Berlin's never been his home.'

I should have been entitled to twenty or thirty thousand marks. At long last, they begrudgingly offered me nine thousand marks from a hardship fund, but five thousand were knocked off straight away for the welfare benefits I'd received when I was ill. I received not a pfennig for my siblings who died in Birkenau, my brother Max, my brother Waldemar, who died in Bialystock, my father, who was also in Bialystock and about whom I'd heard conflicting reports, and for my mother, who died as a result of her time in the concentration camp.

'Prove that she's your mother and that they were your brothers and sisters.'

But I didn't even have my own papers from before, let alone theirs! My birth certificate had been confiscated. I didn't even know the official names of my siblings from my mother's second marriage.

I obtained as many of their papers as I could. 'Okay,' they said, 'there's a way forward. You make a claim on your mother's estate and tell us where she was buried. Then we'll have to exhume her body.'

I don't remember exactly what happened next, I just know that all hell broke loose. I flipped over the desk and some people held me back. 'You fat pigs,' I burst out. 'You're all Nazis. You want me to have my mother exhumed, after all she went through, after losing her children, before you give me this blood money.'

In the end, I just swore off the whole thing. I couldn't deal with it anymore. That was the way it went with so many of us. It didn't help that the Sinti were often illiterate and didn't know their rights.[44]

Back then, I used to go out to Eberswalde and Angermünde to forage for food. If the farmers wouldn't give us anything, we'd wait until evening, go to where the harvested vegetables were stored, fill our potato sacks and leg it. But I didn't just head out there to forage. There were lots of Sinti out there in the forest who would sleep on the farms.

A group of us made our way to Waren an der Müritz and Röbel, where I went to the mayor and said, 'We're looking for our relatives from the concentration camp and will have to stay here overnight. Please could you write a note asking the farmers to give us something to eat?'

Do you think the farmers gave us anything? Of course not. One farmer's neighbour told us: 'That man won't give you any food; he's hidden it all away.' So we went back to the farmer who hadn't wanted to give us anything and said, 'Now listen. We came to you in good faith. We're only asking for a little food so that we can continue on our way. If you don't give it to us, we'll report you to the mayor. We know that you've killed some of your livestock; we know you've got sausage, pork and bacon.' In the end, we got our food. It wasn't much, but it was enough.

In Röbel, I met a girl I liked, a Sinti. But she couldn't keep our relationship a secret and blabbed to her mother, who came and had a word with me. I had to own up, but I liked the girl, and we became an item. She had been in both Ravensbrück and Birkenau. I hadn't noticed her there at the time, but there had been so many people that you could miss someone completely. Besides, we wouldn't have recognized each other – in Auschwitz, we all had shaved heads, but now she had beautiful hair. We were together for seven years.

At first, I lived with her and her mother in Röbel, in a hut in the forest. Various other women from her family lived there, too, and my aunt would visit from Berlin every now and then. Apart from me, the only man about the place was my aunt's husband, Paul

Franzen. There were women everywhere, but no men. That led to some problems with the Russians, who were always after our women.

I would warn them off, saying, '*Nyet, nyet, eta tsiganka eto moya zhena*' – 'No, no, that's my wife!' I wasn't scared of fighting the Russians. We would go at it aggressively. 'That's my wife, and that one, too!'

Uncle Paul would back me up with 'My wife, too, my wife, too.'

'All of them your wife?'

'Yes, all my wife!'

One day, one of them rode into the yard in a carriage. The horses were foaming at the mouth and their necks were soaked with sweat. He was blind drunk. He jumped out, got into a crouch, cocked his rifle and aimed it at me. I'm convinced he would have put a bullet through my head if the rifle hadn't jammed.

For a second, I just stood there, rooted to the spot in shock. Then I came to my senses, ran at him and tore the rifle from his grasp. I snatched up a stone, struck it against the lock, put the cartridge in the right way up, chambered the round and pushed the rifle back into his hands.

'*Togda davay, strelyat*' – 'Go on then, fire!' I tore open my shirt. '*Ya tsygan, ya ne boyus*' – 'I'm a gypsy, I'm not frightened!' And then: '*Ty durnoi ili shto?* – Are you thick or what?'

He threw down the rifle, lurched towards me, engulfed me in an embrace and cried like a little child. '*Ya nie znal, chto ty tsygan!*' He hadn't known that I was a Sinti.

He seemed to have calmed down, but no sooner had I breathed a sigh of relief than he started shooting into the ceiling and the pile of straw in the big hayloft where the women were hiding. I lured him over to the cesspit and snatched his torch off him, tossed away his rifle and gave him a shove, so that he landed in the pit. Then I ran over to the headquarters of his garrison. They questioned me, and in no time the Mongolians were driving over to our place with two cars and a motorbike and sidecar. They grabbed the soldier, gave him a proper beating, threw him into the sidecar and drove off with him like bats out of hell.

When I went over to Röbel a few days later, I passed

by the garrison headquarters. The soldier came to the cellar window and let out a volley of curses so bad I can't possibly repeat them. I just laughed at him.

Everything got cleared up and the Russians never came to our yard again, by order of the commander. 'They're Sinti,' he said. 'They were in a camp.' I had told him who we were and what had happened to us. He wanted us to dance for him. *'Ah! Kharasho!'* he exclaimed happily.

We bought a great big horse and a low-sided cart, and fixed it up with boards at the sides. We sold the horse on to a butcher in Berlin. My mother heard what I was up to and came over to see me. 'You need to get away from there and come back with me,' she said. 'That life isn't for you.'

I returned to Berlin, but I kept pining for the girl. 'Well, what's stopping me going back there?' I thought. I got dressed, left a note on the table for my mother and went back to Röbel. The girl was happy to see me, and so was her mother. We lived in the woods, really, in just a shack, and I had my place by the fire. My suit was full of holes from the flying sparks.

But my mother came after me again. 'Goodness

gracious, boy,' she declared. 'Just look at yourself!' I was like one of those old Sinti men, hunkering around the fire. It was a different sort of life. But I was a city boy really, as my mother-in-law was fond of reminding me.

At one point, I got a particularly beautiful horse in a trade, perfect for riding, named Hansi. I sheared him very short, and when I wanted to hitch him to the cart, he smashed the entire front section. 'Your townie doesn't have a clue!' my mother-in-law said to her daughter.

The horse was no good at pulling carts along the soft forest floor, but as soon as he got onto a paved street he would prance – it was a sight to behold. We needed a workhorse, though, not one for riding. When I took the whip and gave him a crack over the head, he jumped up like a rabbit, and I thought we were done for.

Finally, my mother said, 'Things can't go on like this!' and so I brought the girl to Berlin to live with us. She was completely unsophisticated at the time and still quite young. One time, I tried to take her on the

U-Bahn, but just getting her onto the escalator was a battle in itself. She'd never seen anything like it and simply refused to get on.

She learned quickly, though, and my mother showed her the ropes. Before long, she was as neat and tidy as could be.

We noticed that the butchers in Berlin were buying up horses, so we got into the practice of driving out to the countryside, buying horses, hitching them to our cart, driving back into Berlin and selling them on. We made a good living that way until the authorities brought in contract certificates. That meant that the horse would be given a stamp on its hoof, which had to match up with the certificate, otherwise it couldn't be brought to Berlin. And just like that, our livelihood went up in smoke.

We always drove out in groups and often met Russians out and about with their sturdy little farm horses. They were going about their business, as were we. '*Gde ty rabotayesh?*' they would ask. 'What's your trade?'

'*Artisti*,' we replied – 'We're artists.'

'*A chto ty delayesh?*' – 'What kind?'

OTTO ROSENBERG

'We sing and dance.'

'*Nu davay!*' – 'Go on then, play or sing us something!'

We had our guitars with us. My Uncle Paul was a highly gifted musician, so he would burst into the famous Russian song that begins '*Vykhodila na bereg Katyusha . . .*' They loved it and would dance along.

On one of those occasions, a Russian tried to sell me a horse. I can't remember whether it was a white or a grey one.

'*Wodka yest?*' he said. He wanted to know if I had any vodka.

'*Ja, malo, malo,*' I replied. I had a little.

'*Jaja.*'

So I bought the horse from him for a bottle of vodka.

'*Kharasho!*' Nice doing business with you.

I tethered the horse, and we ate before going our separate ways. I had gone three or four kilometres when I suddenly heard, '*Stoy!*'

'What is it?' I said. 'What's wrong?'

'*Etot kon eto ne tvoi!*' – 'That's not your horse!'

'Who told you that? *Net, eto moy kon.* It is mine.

Your friend sold it to me for a bottle of vodka. *Ya kupil na odnu budelku wodki.'*

'*Ya Kommandant!'* he barked. 'I'm the commander!'

I cursed him in Russian. Some commander he was! He started getting worked up. '*Ladno,'* I said. 'Whatever, you don't scare me. *Ya tsygan, ponimayesh?'*

He changed his tune after that, not least because he didn't have anything to drink either. I scrabbled around for some vodka to give him, and then all was well again.

I often drank with the Russians, knocking back the vodka, with a bit of bacon on the side. They were best buddies when sober, but the moment they got drunk they'd reach for their guns. But after my time in the concentration camp, I wasn't scared of anything, pistols and knives included.

I still have a soft spot for Russians today. Whenever I hear a Russian song, it's like being transported someplace else. They were generous folk. Whenever we came across them, we would say, '*Day mne makhork,'* and they'd reach into their leather trousers and give us tobacco to smoke, even my mother. And if we wanted German newspaper to roll it in, they'd say, '*Germanskaya gazeta ne kharasho, russkaya gazeta, bumaga kharoshaya*' – 'Russian newspaper's much better.'

We were always driving to and fro like that until they brought in the contract certificates and killed our business.

Around the same time, my wife and I split up, too. She wasn't able to have children; they'd messed her up in the camp.[45] Since we weren't a family, there was nothing really keeping us together.

My grandmother was dead, my father was dead, my siblings were dead. There was no one left. I was forced to make big decisions on my own at a very young age. It wasn't easy. Two of my great-uncles, Anton and Florian, were now living in Berlin, so they provided me with some sort of foothold.

It was then that I met the woman who is now my wife, and when she was having our first child, I went to visit my great-uncles in Wittenau.

'Keep your wits about you,' they said. 'Really look at the baby and make sure it's the right one. They swap children at the hospitals, you know.'

'For God's sake, seriously?'

I rang the hospital. 'Hello, Nurse, I have a quick question.' I wasn't married to the mother of my child at this point.

'Yes,' she said, 'the baby's been born. You should be proud. He's a strapping little boy.'

'Hey,' I said to my uncles, 'it's a boy!'

'Well, just be careful,' they said. 'You know what goes on at hospitals.'

So along I went to visit my son. And what do you know, the doctor greeted me with, 'I'm sorry, but there's been a mistake. It's not a son, it's a daughter!'

I was completely confused, I was so young and inexperienced back then. In a stroke of luck, I came by an encyclopaedia, which helped me understand what people were talking about. It was a useful thing to have.

After the birth of my eldest daughter, I spoke to the woman I was still married to, the one who couldn't have children, which had led to us breaking up.

'I have a child now,' I told her.

'Come by with the pram sometime,' she said. 'I want to see her.'

Otto with his wife, Christel, Berlin, 1951

I did as she asked and afterwards, she said, 'If that child had had your eyes, I would have taken her. But she looked back at me with the eyes of that woman. She would always remind me of the concentration camp and of how the Germans made me suffer. And then I'd be raising their children. You belong with the child, not with me.'

I moved into a caravan of my own on Mainzer Straße with the woman who is now my wife and our child. In winter, it was so cold that the little ones had to wear their mittens in bed at night. But we got through it, and eventually I got us an apartment.

My wife and I had seven children, and now we have a few grandchildren, too. She became a stabilizing force in my life. After the awful things that the Germans had done to me, she was good for me. It was difficult at the start, of course. It was a clash of two different worlds, but her kindness and patience with me and the children made things easier. I used to go out and drink a lot when I was young, but later I changed my ways. Go down that road, and you end up hurting your family.

In Hamburg, I got an angel tattooed over my concentration camp number. That degrading number had always bothered me and before I got rid of it, the children were always asking questions about it and wanting to see, so it was a constant reminder. Now the angel's there to guard against that evil and stop it from ever happening again.

I think I was so at odds with God, that He decided to make it back up to me. On 8 June 1953, I married my wife. There were peonies and potato salad, and a little something to eat and drink – a simple affair.

Afterword by Petra Rosenberg

I was born seven years after the liberation of Auschwitz. I have this memory from when I was little: I wake up in the night to hear my father crying loudly, calling out for his siblings and his mother, my grandmother. I stumble drowsily into the kitchen. My father is sitting there. 'Why did they have to die?' he laments. 'Why did I have to be the only one to survive? Those Nazis, those Germans – they killed my whole family. I'm all alone in the world!'

I go to his side, take his hand and weep with him. 'But, Tatta, I'm here for you!' I'm barefoot and freezing, but I can't leave him there like that.

'Oh no, darling, now you're crying. What on earth are you crying for?'

I sob silently. No words come out.

Back then, I didn't get what he was saying. Who were these Nazis who had killed our family? Who were those Germans who wanted to hurt us? And why? What had we done that meant we needed to watch our backs? Why shouldn't we trust them? After all, we were Germans ourselves – weren't we?

No, I couldn't even begin to understand it back then. How could my young mind have conceived of Auschwitz? My father wasn't in the habit of talking about his time in the concentration camps, and I never asked him about it; I didn't want to hurt him.

It took him more than 50 years to put his memories down in writing. So much time has passed, but I'm only just beginning to grasp much of what he wrote. Only now do I have a vague impression, the slightest understanding of the unspeakable torment that was inflicted on the victims. Only now, when my father, too, is gone. What took place back then simply defies comprehension. He writes, 'I wouldn't be able to talk about it now if so many years hadn't passed since. At first, it affected me so badly that I had to stop every three words or so. And I couldn't talk about my parents or brothers and sisters at all . . . On festive occasions, when people gather to celebrate and families meet up, I've often retreated into myself, into my pain. It's very hard.'

The generation who came after them – my generation – were left with severely traumatized mothers and fathers, tormented by their horrific memories and the extermination of their own families.

Over and over, my father would ask himself, 'Why did I survive? How come I made it out of Auschwitz alive? I simply don't know. People say to me, "Hey, at least you're free now – you should be glad!" But all I can think about is my brothers and sisters, and how they were taken, and even now it's hard to find joy in this world.'

Ever since it happened, he has borne witness to those crimes on behalf of the younger generation. I've lost track of how many times my father recounted what he went through. At times, I wondered how he managed to go on living under the weight of such traumatic experiences and memories. Where did he find the strength to embark on a new life after Auschwitz, start a family and throw himself into campaigning for equality for our people? I'm convinced that it was his conviction that there was still something good in people, and his belief in God.

As he saw it, surviving the Auschwitz death camp meant that he had been entrusted with a mission. All those years, he fought for social equality for Sinti and Roma. He was a co-founder and long-standing chairman of the Sinti Union of Berlin and the Berlin-Brandenburg State Association of German Sinti and Roma, which in 1982 banded together with other German Sinti and Roma associations founded in the late 1970s to form the Central Council of German Sinti and Roma.

The civil rights work of these advocacy groups achieved a number of major successes, including the widespread removal of the othering and discriminatory German term *Zigeuner*, at least from official communications. In March 1982, Federal Chancellor Helmut Schmidt officially acknowledged the genocide committed by the Nazis against the Sinti and Roma, in a hugely important step that paved the way for initiatives that would address the genocide at memorial sites and contemporary history museums.

My father campaigned tirelessly for the Marzahn camp to be recognized as a forced labour camp akin to the concentration camps. The Senate of Berlin finally passed a resolution to that effect on 21 July 1987. This meant that all Sinti and Roma who had been interned in Marzahn were recognized by law as having suffered racial persecution under the Nazi regime. He was fiercely committed to having a memorial erected in Berlin to the murdered Sinti and Roma of Europe. It was finally built in 2012.

Although Sinti and Roma were recognized as a national minority in 1995 and their language is included in the European Charter for Regional or Minority Languages, they still encounter rejection in everyday life and face all sorts of economic and professional disadvantages. The widespread acceptance of racist stereotypes and the discrimination and exclusion that come with it, which can include physical violence, only reinforces the ongoing need for the civil rights work by Sinti and Roma groups.

As part of his unflagging quest to educate people and advocate for the social integration of Sinti and Roma, my father organized the Days of Sinti and

Roma Music and Culture in 1992 together with the state of Brandenburg and the International Institute for Comparative Music Studies and Documentation. These events serve as a wide-ranging showcase of the myriad Sinti and Roma cultures worldwide. Underlining the richness of a society where different peoples and ethnic minorities coexist was a crucial part of his efforts towards integration.

As an active member of the Social Democratic Party (SPD), he also initiated discussions in various party committees on the history of persecution and the current situation for Sinti and Roma. He worked with the Young Socialists and the Falcons – the youth wing of the SPD – to organize group trips to former concentration camps and visits to memorial sites, combined with detailed eyewitness reports. He was a steadfast proponent of dialogue between minority and majority populations as a prerequisite for proper reconciliation.

In 1998 my father was awarded the Order of Merit of the Federal Republic of Germany, First Class, for his outstanding achievements in fostering understanding in minority–majority relations. This book was published that same year. He died on 4 July 2001 as a result of the long-term effects of his imprisonment in Nazi concentration camps.

In December 2007, a street and a square were named after him on the historical site of the forced labour camp in Berlin-Marzahn, and in 2011, the Berlin-Marzahn Forced Camp Memorial was erected on that spot. His final resting place was designated a grave of honour by the City of Berlin in July 2016. The Otto-Rosenberg-Haus, a social centre on Otto-Rosenberg-Platz, was opened on 20 August 2020.

On the fortieth anniversary of the Sinti and Roma civil rights movement, Federal President Frank-Walter Steinmeier declared in a video message that 'Our country has a responsibility to remember the crimes against humanity committed by the Nazis. The Berlin memorial commemorating the Sinti and Roma of Europe who were murdered between 1933 and 1945 represents an ongoing undertaking for the state and society at large.' And he raised something new: 'Today, on behalf of our country, I want to ask forgiveness for the second wave of suffering inflicted on the Sinti and Roma during the post-war period.'

Tragically, the darkest chapter in German history is now deeply interwoven into the history of our people. It informs how all European Sinti and Roma see the present and has left a lasting imprint not only on the survivors, but also on the generations that have come after them.

In his memoir, *A Gypsy in Auschwitz*, my father bears witness to his odyssey through the concentration camps. It is a story that urgently needs to be told, because the history of persecution suffered by the victims of the Nazis is at its most immediate and explicit when expressed through the fate of the individual.

April 2022

Endnotes

1. Rosenberg or von Rosenberg is one of the earliest Sinti surnames documented in Germany from the early 15th century onwards. One Johannes Rosenberg, a Prussian soldier and *tschatschopaskero*, or leader of the Brandenburg Sinti, was at the centre of the trial over the 'Gypsy conspiracy in Prussia', which ended in an acquittal (Reimar Gilsenbach, *Tschuttemann. Exposé*, 1997, and the same author's *Oh Django, sing deinen Zorn!*, Berlin 1993, p. 65).

2. The Berlin-Marzahn concentration camp, which was the first racially defined forced labour camp in Nazi Germany, was established without any legal grounds by the Berlin police chief and the city administration, with the agreement of the Office of Racial Policy of the Nazi Party (NSDAP). On 16 June 1936, the *Berliner Lokal-Anzeiger* newspaper ran a piece with the headline 'Berlin ohne Zigeuner' ('Berlin without Gypsies') (Joachim S Hohmann, *Verfolgte ohne Heimat. Geschichte der Zigeuner in Deutschland*, pp. 70–1 and Gilsenbach, *Oh Django*, p. 142). Hardened Nazi official Gerhard Stein inspected the Marzahn camp prior to 26 October 1936 on behalf of the Berlin police chief. Stein believed that the gypsies had a king until 1918 and declared that 'the Gypsy bastard' was 'the worst and most inferior being imaginable [....] brutish and truculent, workshy and mendacious, dishonest and dirty and prone to drunkenness, politically utterly objectionable, of course, and wholly idle apart from efforts to instigate trouble'. Yet even Stein could not avoid the conclusion that the forced settlement had torn the inmates away from their trades and made them destitute.

In his report, he also notes: 'The place is in the immediate vicinity of sewage farms, which emit dreadful fumes that are unbearable at times, especially in the evening and in certain weather conditions. Despite undergoing tests, the water from the newly drilled well is, in fact, undrinkable, so the people are accustomed to fetching their water from the nearby village. Worst of all are the toilet facilities, which are wholly inadequate for such a large number of people. I am convinced that the place is rife with disease' (Federal Archives, Berlin-Lichterfelde external branch, Record 142, Annex 29).

3. In November 1936, the Racial Hygiene and Demographic Biology Research Institute of the Public Health Department began work in Berlin-Dahlem, with Dr Robert Ritter as its director. Ritter established one of the key prerequisites for the holocaust of the Sinti and Roma by deeming 'part-Gypsies' – as opposed to 'racially pure Gypsies' – 'genetically inferior' and characterizing them as 'highly maladjusted, lacking in character, wayward, unreliable and sluggish or unsettled and irascible'. Elsewhere, he branded them 'workshy and asocial' (Karin Reemtsma, *Sinti und Roma: Geschichte, Kultur, Gegenwart,* Munich 1996, pp. 103–4).

A 42-page 'genealogy' of the Hamburg and Berlin branch of the Rosenberg family outlined by Ritter and presumably fleshed out by Eva Justin demonstrates his working methods. Otto Rosenberg's great-grandparents have only brief mentions, as 'Tschamperdis Freiwald' and 'Reina Klemens'. This supposed genealogical account was drawn up as a means of registering the family, with the sole purpose of marking them for extermination (Federal Archive, Berlin-Lichterfelde branch, Record 165, Annexes 160–120). In March 1942, Ritter and his assistants registered some 21,498 'Gypsies and part-Gypsies'. Their 'genealogies' and 'expert statements' served as the basis for the almost complete annihilation of these people (Reemtsma, *Sinti und Roma*, p. 105).

4. A commemorative event, led by Otto's daughter, Petra Rosenberg, is still held on this date every year at the Berlin-Marzahn Forced Camp Memorial.

5. Ritter, who rose to become director of the Public Health Department of the Reich in 1944, was appointed director of the Welfare Office for Patients with Emotional and Nervous Disorders and Paediatric Psychiatry in Frankfurt am Main after the war. In 1948, he brought Justin, who had been deemed 'politically blameless' in the denazification proceedings, on board to work with him as a 'criminal psychologist'. All subsequent proceedings against the two were dropped (Reemtsma, *Sinti und Roma*, pp. 130–1). Leo Karsten remained with the Criminal Investigation Bureau and was transferred to Karlsruhe (ibid., p. 126).

6. Under the directives of the Asocial Decree issued by the Minister of the Interior on 4 April 1938, 'travellers (Gypsies)' were deemed asocial, even if they had a sufficient income and no previous convictions. The transfer of men from Marzahn to the concentration camp at Sachsenhausen was part of a larger wave of detentions (Reemtsma, *Sinti und Roma*, p. 90).

7. According to Wilhelm Stuckart and Hans Globke in *Kommentare zur deutschen Rassengesetzgebung*, vol. I, Berlin 1936, 'Jews and Gypsies' were 'members of alien races'. The First Implementing Regulations for the Genetic Purity Law of 14 November 1935 had already denied 'Gypsies' German citizenship and forbidden intermarriages (Stuckart and Globke, *Kommentare*, pp. 88–9).

8. The Kriminalpolizei (criminal police) oversaw the Berlin-Marzahn camp and various other 'Gypsy community camps'. In 1936, the Reich Criminal Police Department set up the Central Office for Combatting the Gypsy Menace, which in turn oversaw the newly formed Office for Gypsy Affairs at the Kriminalpolizei headquarters (Stuckart and Globke, *Kommentare*, p. 89). This body was tasked with 'ensuring that Gypsies did not use the trams, keep pets, visit taverns, have sexual relations with those of "German blood", or receive any poste restante letters' (ibid., p. 107).

9. Leo Karsten was in charge of the Office for Gypsy Affairs in Berlin. His card index and a few of his files are stored in the State Archives in Potsdam, under Pr. Br. Rep. 30 Berlin C Tit 198a 3. Zigeuner.

10. Otto Rosenberg's grandmother Charlotte Rosenberg was an extra in the film *Tiefland*, starring Leni Riefenstahl. As filmmaker Nina Gladitz revealed in her film *Time of Darkness and Silence* (1982), in 1941–2 Riefenstahl picked a number of Sinti from the Maxglan concentration camp near Salzburg to work on the film. The extras were under police guard during the shoot and did not receive any direct payment (judgment at Freiburg District Court, 25 June 1985). Riefenstahl brought a case against Gladitz, in which she presented a bill showing that Sinti from the Berlin-Marzahn camp were also used on the *Tiefland* set from 27 April 1942 onwards. 'On 6 April 1943, Riefenstahl-Film GmbH paid 3,060.45 Marks as a 15 per cent "social levy" for 68 "Gypsies" from Marzahn. Almost all of the Sinti on the list were deported to the Auschwitz-Birkenau extermination camp in early March 1943 – a month before Riefenstahl settled her bill' (Gilsenbach, *Oh Django*, p. 167). After the war, Riefenstahl won a series of lawsuits relating

to this matter, during which she called Maxglan 'a relief and welfare camp'. At one of those trials in 1949, her legal team called the former camp commander, SS Sturmbannführer and detective superintendent Anton Böhmer as an expert witness, who stated that, 'The Salzburg/Maxglan camp was never under SS command, SS guards or under the slightest SS influence, not for a single second. I categorically reject any assertion to the contrary as a gross distortion of the truth and a barefaced lie!' (*Anton Böhmer, expert witness in the trial of Leni Riefenstahl vs. the publisher Kindler in Munich, 1949*, photocopy, Nina Gladitz Filmproduktion, Kirchzarten 1985).

11. On 13 March 1942, the Minister for Labour decreed that the 'special regulations under social law' that were enacted against the Jews should also be applied to 'Gypsies' (Gilsenbach, *Oh Django*, p. 90).

12. On 16 December 1942, Himmler ordered the deportation of 'Gypsy half-breeds' to the Auschwitz concentration camp (Gilsenbach, *Oh Django*, p. 90). The Berlin-Marzahn camp was broken up on 1 March 1943 and almost all of its inmates deported to the Gypsy Camp at Auschwitz-Birkenau (ibid., p. 179). Two families remained in the camp, having been deemed by Ritter to be 'pure-blooded Sinti and Lalleri Gypsies'. In accordance with Himmler's plans, these families were to be resettled on a reserve in Ödenburg on Lake Neusiedl, along with seven other families (ibid., p. 155).

13. 14 April 1943: 'A transport of Gypsies arrived from the territory of the Reich. Twenty men and boys were given numbers Z-6071 to Z-6090 ...' (Danuta Czech, *Kalendarium der Ereignisse im Konzentrationslager Auschwitz-Birkenau 1939–1945*, Reinbek 1989, p. 468). Entry in the 'Hauptbuch

des Zigeunerlagers' (main registry for the Gypsy Camp): '(consecutive numbering) 6084, (reason for detention) Zig. D. R. (Zigeuner Deutsches Reich (Gypsy of the German Reich), (surname) Rosenberg, (first name) Otto, (date of birth) 28/4/27, (place of birth) Stallupöhnen, (day of admission to the camp) 14/4/43, (notes) (Birk.) (18/5/43)' (cited in *Gedenkbuch. Die Sinti und Roma im KZ Auschwitz-Birkenau*, Munich 1993, vol. 2).

The main registry for the Gypsy Camp survived thanks to the bravery of Polish political prisoners and report writers Tadeusz Joachimowski and Ireneusz Pietrzyk and their fellow prisoner Henryk Porebski, who in July 1944, as the planned destruction of the camp approached, sneaked it out of the camp office, wrapped it in clothing, concealed it in a bucket and buried it between Barrack 31 and the fence of the BIId camp, where the men were kept. It was recovered from its burial spot on 13 January 1949 by employees of the Auschwitz State Memorial, with Tadeusz Joachimowski present (*Gedenkbuch*, vol. I, p. xxxvii).

14. 'The Nazis would sometimes spare boys and use them as apprentice bricklayers for the construction of the crematoria in Birkenau. This work crew was dubbed the Maurerschule [bricklaying school]' (Ota Kraus and Erich Kulka, *Die Todesfabrik Auschwitz*, Berlin 1991, pp. 147–8).

15. 26 February 1943: 'The first transport of Gypsies from the German Reich were sent to the Auschwitz concentration camp on 29 January 1943, following the decree by the Reich Security Head Office; some men, women and children arrived. They were accommodated in the camp in the yet-to-be-completed BIIe section of Birkenau, which would be called the BIIe Gypsy Camp' (Czech, *Kalendarium*, p. 423).

16. 'These were OKH-type 260/9 stable huts originally designed for 52 horses. In Birkenau, each one housed 400 inmates or more' (*Gedenkbuch*, p. 371).

17. The following were recorded in the main register for men: Florian R., number 2725, 13 March 1943; Oskar R., number 4858, 19 March 1943; Werner August (Bodo) R., number 4860, 19 March 1943; Albert R., number 4976, 24 March 1943; Henry R., number 5455, 28 March 1943; and Anton R., number 9864, 24 May 1944. The main register for women contains entries for Charlotte R. (number 5406) and Therese R. (number 5407), but the day on which they were admitted to the camp is not recorded.

18. 'On 10 July 1942, the High Command of the Wehrmacht ordered that "Gypsies" and "part-Gypsies" be dismissed from the military for "reasons of racial policy"' (Reemtsma, *Sinti und Roma*, p. 107). In his account, Auschwitz Commander Rudolf Höss writes that 'Many men were detained while on leave from the front, despite being decorated soldiers or having been wounded multiple times, simply because their father or mother or grandfather had been a Gypsy or a Gypsy half-caste' (*KL Auschwitz in den Augen der SS. Höß/Broad/Kremer*, Verlag des Staatlichen Auschwitz-Museums 1973, p. 64).

19. Kapo was the name given to the prisoner-supervisors who oversaw the forced labour in the camps. The word may be derived from the Italian for leader or head, *capo*.

20. 'The penal block (penal company) was Block 2 in BIId, the main men's camp, where the Jews were. This directly adjoined

the Gypsy Camp [...] The prisoners in this block had a big black dot on the front and back of their clothing, while those who were thought to be at risk of attempting to escape also had a big red circle' (Ota Kraus and Erich Kulka, *Die Todesfabrik Auschwitz*, pp. 91–2).

21. SS Untersturmführer Hans Schwarzhuber became the first director of the BIId men's camp on 22 November 1943 (Czech, *Kalendarium*, p. 659).

22. 'The "sauna" was built in late 1943, with a shower room and disinfection facilities for clothing' (Tadeusz Szymański, Danuta Szymańska and Tadeusz Śnieszko, 'Das "Spital" im Zigeuner-Familienlager in Auschwitz-Birkenau', in *Die Auschwitz-Hefte*, vol. I, ed. Hamburg Institute of Social Research, Weinheim and Basel 1987, p. 201).

23. Lucie Adelsberger, an inmate who began working as a camp doctor at the Gypsy Camp on 21 May 1943, also recalls this 'well-meaning kapo' in her book *Auschwitz: A Doctor's Story* (Boston, MA, 1995): 'This man was a German, a victim of political persecution, and you couldn't meet anyone kinder. In the camp, water was supposed to be used sparingly, and administered with beatings, but he let the warm streams of water gush over us' (p. 86).

24. According to Ritter's genealogical record, Otto's mother, Elisabeth (Luise) Rosenberg, became a Freiwald when she married her second husband. Paul Freiwald, born 26 October 1937 in Versen, was her only son from her second marriage. He was recorded in the main register with this name and date of birth, plus 'Fursen, Rhineland' as his place of birth.

Veronika Freiwald was entered in the main register for women as number 249, and Rosa Freiwald as number 250. The day they were admitted to the camp is not recorded. The date of Veronika's death is illegible, while that of Rosa (who was registered as Sophie) is only partially legible (2/?/44).

25. 'After Mengele sent a group of patients with typhus to the gas chambers in May 1943, he never again selected those suffering from the disease. Instead, he ordered "delousing operations" in the infirmary and the barracks. In the infirmary, this involved pulling severely ill patients from their plank beds and laying them on the smoke-vent oven while the blankets and sacks of straw were sent to the "sauna" for disinfection. [...] Delousing operations within the camp followed more or less the same sequence, but along with the disinfection of clothing and bedding, the Gypsies were also forced to bathe in the sauna and could only re-enter the barracks once the delousing operation was complete. Sometimes it took from morning to evening' (Szymański et al., 'Das "Spital" im Zigeuner-Familienlager in Auschwitz-Birkenau', p. 203).

26. 'These men and women worked in the complex of buildings that we called "Kanada". When new inmates arrived at the camp, they were forced to abandon their possessions as soon as they got off the train, and they were taken off to be stored in "Kanada". [...] The things that the Kanada Kommando managed to appropriate could enhance life in the camp quite considerably' (Adelsberger, *Auschwitz: A Doctor's Story*, p. 75). 'And then there was another crew whose specific task earned them the name of Sonderkommando ["special kommando"] [...] This group had the horrific job of working in the crematorium. As far as we could make out, these inmates had to gather up everything that the unfortunate souls who

were about to be sent to the gas had brought with them into the death chamber – their clothing and every last personal belonging [...] They sometimes came into our bit of the camp to bathe [...] One they had done this job for a few months at most, they were themselves sent to the gas chambers, to ensure that word would never get out' (ibid., p. 79).

27. 'We weren't meant to know about the existence of the crematoria. Our mother taught us what to say if the SS asked us about it. We were supposed to say, "That chimney and oven over there is for making the bread we eat every day." But everyone knew what it was really for' (Ceija Stojka, *Wir leben im Verborgenen. Erinnerungen einer Rom-Zigeunerin*, ed. Karin Berger, Vienna 1989, pp. 27–8).

28. Mengele had an office at the sauna (Szymański et al., 'Das "Spital" im Zigeuner-Familienlager in Auschwitz-Birkenau', p. 205).

29. 25 May 1943: 'The SS camp doctor for the Gypsy Camp in Birkenau ordered a camp lockdown, during which 507 male Gypsies with numbers Z-7666 to Z-8178 and 528 female Gypsies with numbers Z-8331 to Z-8864 were to be sent to the gas chambers. Among them were a number of inmates with typhus and another several hundred suspected of suffering from the disease.' A comparison of the selected inmate numbers with the main register reveals that the murdered prisoners mainly came from Poland, including many from Białystock and Suwałki, and from Russia (Czech, *Kalendarium*, p. 503).

30. 15 May 1944: 'The command at Auschwitz has made the decision to liquidate the inhabitants of the Blle Gypsy Family

Camp in Birkenau the very next day. This camp housed around six thousand men, women and children. The camp leader for the BIIe section at that time was Paul Bonigut, who was opposed to this decision. He passed on the information in secret to certain Gypsies whom he trusted, so that they wouldn't let themselves be slaughtered like sheep.' 16 May 1944: 'At around seven o'clock in the evening, a lockdown was announced at the Blle Family Camp in Birkenau. Trucks pulled up outside and SS guards armed with machine guns jumped out and encircled the camp. The man in charge ordered the Gypsies to leave their barracks. Having been forewarned, the Gypsies had armed themselves with knives, shovels, crowbars and rocks, and refused to leave their barracks. Surprised, the SS went off to the block leader's office to consult with the official in charge of the operation. After a discussion, a whistle was blown to signal that the SS teams who had surrounded the barracks should withdraw. The SS left the camp. The first attempt to liquidate the Gypsies had failed' (Czech, *Kalendarium*, pp. 774–5).

31. 23 May 1944: 'More than 1,500 Gypsies – men, women and children – were now housed in Blocks 10 and 11 of the main camp, following the failed attempt by the SS to liquidate the Blle Gypsy Family Camp in Birkenau. Those selected were to be transferred to other concentration camps within the Reich' (Czech, *Kalendarium*, p. 781).2 August 1944:

    'In the afternoon, an empty goods train was made ready in the railway siding at Birkenau. Some 1,408 Gypsy men and women from the BIIe camp and Blocks 10 and 11 of the main camp were separated out and brought to the railway ramp. They were to remain alive, so they were being transferred to other concentration camps. Those departing said goodbye through the fence to the Gypsies who would remain behind in the BIIe camp through the fence. At around seven o'clock in the evening, the train pulled away from the ramp at Birkenau, bound for the Buchenwald concentration camp' (ibid., p. 838).

'After evening rollcall, a camp lockdown was ordered in Auschwitz II and the BIIe Gypsy Family Camp. The BIIe camp and a few other barracks that still housed some Gypsies were surrounded by armed SS. Trucks drove into the camp and the guards herded 2,897 defenceless men, women and children onto them and drove them to the gas chambers at the crematorium. After the gassing, the corpses of the murdered Gypsies were burned in the pit next to the crematorium, as the ovens were not working at the time' (ibid., p. 838).

32. 3 August 1944: 'The transport containing the Gypsies from Auschwitz II, Birkenau, arrived at Buchenwald. It comprised 918 Gypsies, including 105 boys aged 9 to 14, 393 youths aged 15 to 24, 330 men aged 25 to 44, 59 men aged 45 to 64; two men aged over 65, one man whose age is not given, and five men who were not included in the list. The women were presumably sent to subcamps' (Czech, *Kalendarium*, p. 840).

'Of the total 4,183 prisoners who were transferred from the Gypsy Camp to other camps, [...] it is necessary to subtract the 1,800 Gypsies who were sent back to Auschwitz and killed in the gas chambers' (Szymański et al., 'Das "Spital" im Zigeuner-Familienlager in Auschwitz-Birkenau', p. 207).

33. Following the destruction of the V1 and V2 rocket manufacturing facilities in Peenemünde in a British air raid on 17–18 August 1943, prisoners were brought in trucks from Buchenwald to Nordhausen in the southern Harz region during the night of 27–28 August 1943, to be used as labour to expand an existing tunnel system within the Kohnstein hill (Erhard Pachaly and Kurt Eund Pelny, *KZ Mittelbau-Dora*,

Berlin 1990, pp. 7–8). The aim was to set up a factory capable of producing 1,800 rockets per month (ibid., p. 65). By December 1943, 10,475 prisoners were already working at this camp (ibid., p. 68). Around two hundred prisoners died every day, some of them in mass hangings from overhead cranes (ibid., pp. 72–3). After the initial series of VI drops on English cities in the second half of June 1944, there was a drop in mortality at the camp.

In August 1944, around a hundred of the roughly twelve thousand prisoners died (ibid., p. 95). On 28 October 1944, the camp, now numbering fifteen thousand men, was renamed the Mittelbau-Dora Concentration Camp and declared officially separate from Buchenwald (*Das nationalsozialistische Lagersystem (CCP)*, ed. Martin Weinmann, Frankfurt am Main 2001, pp. 565 and 739).

'There were a great many Gypsies in the Mittelbau-Dora concentration camp. According to the statistics, it contained 1,185 Gypsies on 1 November 1944. On 20 February 1945 there were 365 inmates wearing a black triangle in the Ellrich satellite camp, and 479 in the Harzungen satellite camp on 15 December 1944. This indicates that there were four to five thousand Gypsies in Dora and its external outposts' (Pachaly and Pelny, *KZ Mittelbau-Dora*, p. 111).

34. The outpost of the Dora-Mittelbau camp at Ellrich, Nord-hausen, was created on 2 May 1944 as 'Mittelbau II', and given the codename 'Erich'. It had an average capacity of 8,000 prisoners (Pachaly and Pelny, *KZ Mittelbau-Dora*, p. 569).

35. Construction on the BIII site in Woffleben began beneath the Himmelsberg in 1944–45 (Pachaly and Pelny, *KZ Mittelbau-Dora*, p. 169). Among other things, this was intended for production of the secret weapons known as the 'Taifun',

'Schmetterling' and 'Eidechse'. By the end of September 1944, 2,660 prisoners were working here. 'The aim was to increase the number of prisoners for the intended measures and special production to around 5,320, but only some of those prisoners could be accommodated in the Woffleben barracks. This meant that the majority of the prisoner crews had to come from the Ellrich camp complex' (ibid., pp. 173–4).

36. 'The Jews were assigned the hardest work […] The SS liked to order the Jews to work on the "terrace" – i.e. above ground. They dug ditches for the water supply system or for the installation of sewage channels. They also used them to level the ground and work of that nature' (Pachaly and Pelny, *KZ Mittelbau-Dora*, p. 110).

37. 'Monthly report from the inmate infirmary at the Erich work camp from 21/12/1944 to 20/1/1945: "Due to the scarce supply of shoes, there is a notable prevalence of frostbite of the lower extremities, which is difficult to treat due to the pronounced lack of bandages."' Of the 6,975 prisoners, 513 died over this period (Pachaly and Pelny, *KZ Mittelbau-Dora*, pp. 252–3).

38. Ibid.: 'Camp Erich is completely ridden with lice. Delousing is currently ongoing […] Unfortunately, we cannot expect any great success, as only 200 balls of wood shavings were provided, and new straw sacks could not be delivered to replace the old ones.'

39. A witness to an execution in Dora-Mittelbau recounts that 'The seven prisoners had a wooden gag stuck in their mouths, which was then fixed at the back with a wire, so that they couldn't speak or cry out' (Pachaly and Pelny, *KZ Mittelbau-Dora*, p. 99).

40. SS Obersturmführer Oskar Dirlewanger was the commander of a 'voluntary' SS brigade of concentration camp inmates, preferably from the Reich and released on a probationary basis.

41. On 1 January 1945, there were 18,465 people imprisoned in Bergen-Belsen. By 1 March, this number had risen to 41,520 due to the evacuation of concentration camps closer to the front. 'In the month of March, mortality in the camp was so unbelievably high (as mentioned above, 18,168 people died in that month alone) that the camp population did not increase significantly, despite the transports constantly pouring in' (Eberhard Kolb, *Bergen-Belsen. Vom 'Aufenthaltslager' zum Konzentrationslager 1943–1945*, Göttingen 1985, p. 40).

    The transports from the Dora-Mittelbau camp arrived in around the second week in April. 'This camp and its many external outposts were cleared from 4 April due to the approach of the American troops; an estimated twenty-five to thirty thousand Dora inmates reached Bergen-Belsen in around ten freight trains after several days of constant travelling, often interrupted by air raids, diversions and traffic congestion. However, these transports were not accommodated in the camp itself, but in the barracks at the nearby military training ground' (Kolb, *Bergen-Belsen*, p. 41). The last sentence explains why Otto remembers large stone barracks, which were different to those in the prisoner enclosure of the camp proper.

42. Himmler was persuaded to have the camp handed over to the British, rather than evacuated as the other camps near the front had been. 'The ceasefire agreement signed on the night of 12–13 April provided for the neutralisation of a rectangular parcel of land 8km long and 6km wide around the Bergen-Belsen camp, and also stipulated that until the camp

was taken over by British troops, it would be supervised by
soldiers in the German Wehrmacht and a unit of Hungarian
soldiers, rather than the SS. The remaining soldiers would
be free to withdraw to German lines with their weapons,
equipment and vehicles within six days. The wording of the
ceasefire agreement was rather vague on the subject of the SS
command [...] In actual fact, the majority of the SS departed
on 13 April, while Kramer stayed behind in Bergen-Belsen
with around 50 SS guards and 30 female SS overseers' (Kolb,
Bergen-Belsen, pp. 48–9).

'Frenzied scenes took place on the day of liberation and the
following night [...] SS and Wehrmacht guards fired into the
crowd, killing countless people; a number of loathed kapos
were lynched [...] The first major British medical unit entered
Bergen-Belsen on 17 April [...] The evacuation of the camp
began on 24 April. Both the sick and those who were still
reasonably healthy were now transferred to the barracks of the
military training ground [...]' (Kolb, *Bergen-Belsen*, pp. 50–1).

Despite the utmost efforts to save the survivors, around
13,000 people died even after they had been liberated (*Bergen-Belsen. Texte und Bilder der Ausstellung in der zentralen
Gedenkstätte des Landes Niedersachsen auf dem Gelände
des ehemaligen Konzentrations- und Kriegsgefangenenlagers
Bergen-Belsen*, ed. Centre for Political Education, Hanover
Hameln 1990, p. iv/I).

43. The Frontkämpfersiedlung 'Schlageter' (Schlageter estate
for front-line veterans) was inaugurated on 1 August 1934
(Neuköllner Kulturverein e. V., *Vom Ilsenhof zum Highdeck.
Modelle sozialen Wohnens in Neukölln*, ed. Brigitte Jacob and
Harald Ramm, Berlin 1987, p. 101).

44. Otto Rosenberg only knew the Sinti names of his half-sisters from his mother's second marriage – Traubela, Buchela and Reibkuchen. He did not have access to Ritter's 'genealogy', where the names are jotted in in pencil and appear alongside their official names, Veronika (born 29 October 1934) and Rosa (born 26 February 1936), together with the entry for Otto's half-brother, Paul. Ritter had given these and all of his other 'genealogies' to Eva Justin, who handed them over to employees from the 'Central Office for Traveller Affairs' at the Bavarian State Bureau of Criminal Investigations in 1949. After they had been used for a number of years, the genealogies were passed on to Professor Hermann Arnold, then at the Institute of Anthropology at the University of Mainz. Following protests by the Society for Threatened Peoples, they were finally confiscated by the Federal Archives in 1981 (Letter from lawyer Hartmut Wächtler and others to Munich I District Court, dated 13 March 1984).

'When ruling upon persecuted persons' applications for compensation, the courts consulted former employees of the "Office for Gypsy Affairs" at the Reich Security Head Office and the Racial Hygiene Research Centre at the Reich Ministry of Health' (Reemtsma, *Sinti und Roma*, p. 133).

According to a ruling by the Federal Court of Justice, 'Gypsies' were only persecuted for racial reasons from 1943 onwards. This decision was revised in 1963. The deadline for persecuted people to apply for compensation expired on 31 December 1969. In 1981, the German federal government issued new guidelines for 'compensation for hardship in individual cases for persecuted persons of non-Jewish origin'. However, 'only those who had never submitted an application for compensation were eligible to apply. Sinti and Roma whose applications had previously been rejected under the old jurisdiction were not entitled to the paltry maximum sum of

5,000 Deutschmarks, or to a meagre pension' (Reemtsma, *Sinti und Roma*, p. 134).

45. Concentration camp doctors such as the gynaecologist Professor Carl Clauberg devised X-ray procedures and other techniques that allowed them to carry out a thousand sterilisations a day. 'They mainly conducted their experiments on "Gypsy women" imprisoned in the Auschwitz-Birkenau concentration camp. In March 1945, a few weeks before the end of the war, Clauberg sterilised 20 Sinti girls in the Ravensbrück concentration camp' (Gilsenbach, *Oh Django*, pp. 82–3).